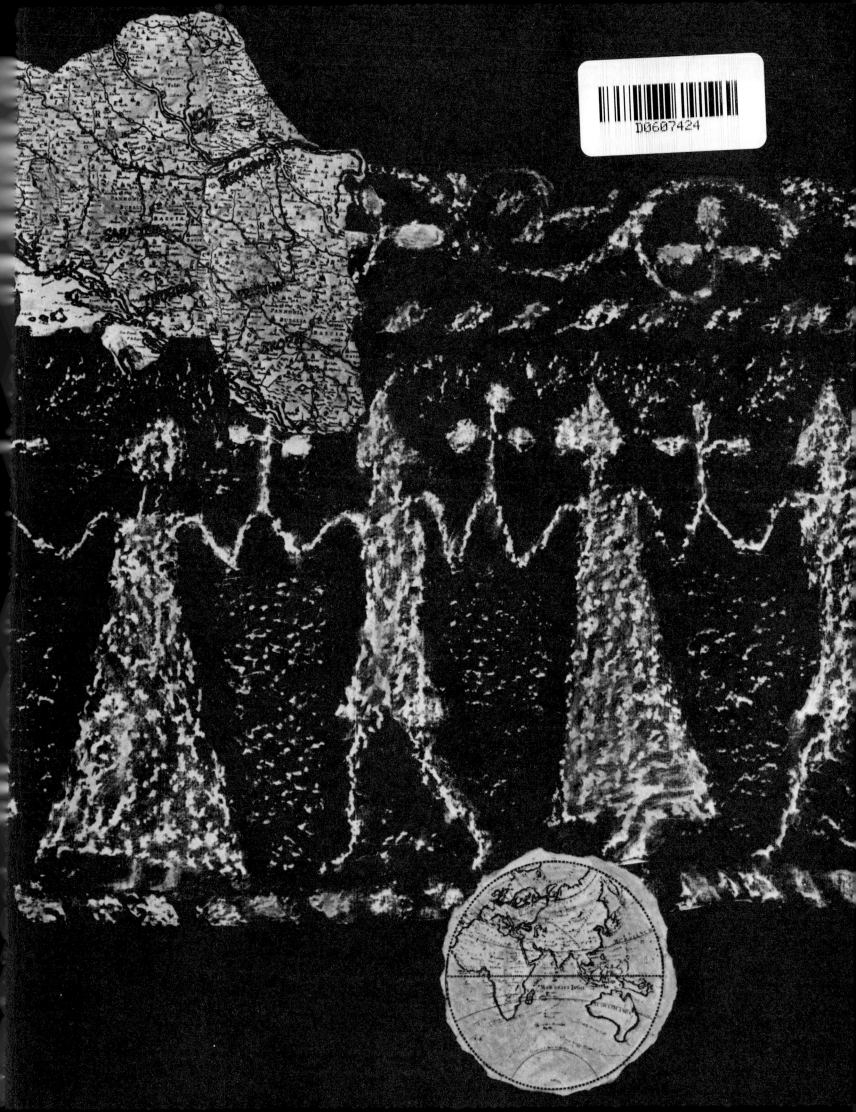

YUGOSLAVIA

YUGOSLAVIA, REPUBLICS AND PROVINCES

Published by
JUGOSLOVENSKA REVIJA
Terazije 31, Belgrade
Director and Editor-in-Chief
RAJKO BOBOT

Editorial Board
Vukašin MIĆUNOVIĆ, chairman
Nikola BAN
Rajko BOBOT
Tihomir ILIJEVSKI
Veljko KOJOVIĆ
Vojislav MIĆOVIĆ
Jorgovanka MILOJEVIĆ
Olga PEROVIĆ
Radoman PERKOVIĆ
Aleksandar PETKOVIĆ
Marjan ŠIFTAR

Editorial consultants
Svetozar KRUNIĆ
Dragoljub VUJICA

Translator
Madge PHILLIPS TOMAŠEVIĆ

Editor
Miša ŠPILJEVIĆ

Designer
Miodrag VARTABEDIJAN

YUGOSLAVIA

*Republics
and
Provinces*

JUGOSLOVENSKA
REVIJA

Authors
Vukašin MIĆUNOVIĆ, Introduction
Veljko KOJOVIĆ
Milo KRALJ
Auguštin LAH
Miroslav MARKOVIĆ
Milutin MIJANOVIĆ
Mirko PERŠEN
Dušan POPOV
Kosta RAKIĆ
Ivan TOŠEVSKI

Photographs:
Rafaelo BENCINI
Ilijas BEŠIĆ
Kiro BILBILOVSKI
Budim BUDIMOVSKI
Aleksandar CVETINOVSKI
Blagoje DRNKOV
Miodrag DJORDJEVIĆ
Ivo ETEROVIĆ
Nenad GATTIN
Mladen GRČEVIĆ
Duško JOVANOVIĆ
Voja JOVANOVIĆ
Slobodan KRSTANOVIĆ
Dimitrije MANOLEV
Mihailo MATIĆ
Slobodan MILETIĆ
Dragan MILANOVIĆ
Milenko NEŠKOVIĆ
Ivo PERVAN
Tomislav PETERNEK
Djordje POPOVIĆ
Radoslav RANISAVLJEVIĆ
Branislav STRUGAR
Boris VUKASOVIĆ
Dragoljub ZAMUROVIĆ
Vilko ZUBAR
Joco ŽNIDARŠIČ
Photographic archives of
JUGOSLOVENSKA REVIJA

Proof-reader
Vladimir RISTIĆ

A MOTOVUN BOOK
Copyright 1986, Jugoslovenska revija, Belgrade

Printed in 20,000 copies
Separate editions in Serbo-Croatian,
English, German and French

Printed by
GORENJSKI TISK, KRANJ, 1986

CONTENTS

The Socialist Federal Republic of Yugoslavia occupies 2.6 % of the area of Europe between 40° 51′ and 46° 53′ latitude north, and 13° 23′ and 23° 02′ longitude east. Three-quarters of its territory lies in the north-west and central part of the Balkan peninsula, and the rest in the southern part of central Europe. Confronted by various interpretations of the history of the numerous tribes, peoples and nations which have struggled to assert their identity and create their states in the Balkans, teachers tell their pupils that their homeland is a Central European, Balkan and Mediterranean country. The river Danube, which receives 120 tributaries as it flows through Yugoslavia, was once the frontier between the Roman Empire and barbarian peoples.

With an area of 255,804 km², Yugoslavia is ninth in size among the European states. Its geological structure is extremely complex, with all types of sedimentary and various magmatic and metamorphic rocks. This geological structure accounts for the discovery of considerable quantities of lignite and brown coal, petroleum and natural gas, thermal waters and various ores — iron, copper, zinc, lead, aluminium, silver, gold, mercury and other metals. Yugoslavia is predominantly a mountainous land — 70.5 % is over 200 m above sea level. Pedologists have identified 36 types of soil. The lowland regions, mainly the Pannonian Plain and valleys of the Sava, Drava, Morava, Drina, Vardar, Neretva, Zeta and other rivers, are sown with maize, wheat, rice, cotton and other industrial crops and medicinal plants. The highlands have extensive pastures and forests, favouring the development of livestock breeding and the timber industry. Most of the Balkan coast of the Adriatic Sea, from the Bay of Trieste to the mouth of the river Bojana, with a total length of 2,092 km, belongs to Yugoslavia. The actual coastline, if we include the 66 inhabited islands, 645 isles and 517 large rocks, amounts to 6,116 km. The rivers, which drain into the Black, Adriatic or Aegean Seas, have considerable power and navigation potential. The coast, mountains, river gorges and lakes make this a land of exceptional scenic beauty. Many of the most outstanding areas are included in the 19 national parks.

A moderate continental climate prevails over most of the country. The influence of mountains, rivers and other factors account for its variability and local differences. The coastal belt and south of the country enjoy a mild Mediterranean climate. The varied climatic conditions allow the cultivation of olives, vines, figs, tobacco, plums and a wide variety of other fruit and vegetables. The mountains and woodlands have an abundance of wild life.

The Socialist Federal Republic of Yugoslavia borders in the north on Austria (324 km of frontier) and Hungary (623 km), in the north-east on Romania (557 km), in the east on Bulgaria (536 km), in the south on Greece (262 km) and Albania (465 km), and in the west and south-west on Italy (202 km). In each of these countries there are Yugoslav national minorities, just as in this country there are people who belong by ethnic origin to neighbouring nations (the most numerous are Albanians and Hungarians). Respecting the inviolability of the frontiers with neighbouring states established after the Second World War, Yugoslavia in its Constitution and laws has laid down the rights of the nationalities (i.e. national minorities) living within its borders, which go far beyond just the use of their mother tongue and cultural autonomy. There is consistent respect of the constitutional principle that "work and the results of work determine the material and social position of the individual, on the basis of equal rights and responsibilities, regardless of nationality, sex and attitude to religion".

In size of population, Yugoslavia takes eighth place in Europe. At the time of the 1981 census it had 22,424,711 inhabitants, of whom 11,340,000 were women and 11,100,000 men. This was over 6.5 million more than in 1948. The average density is 88 persons per square kilometre. Serbia is the most densely populated (105.4 per 1 km^2), and Montenegro the least (42.3).

The history of the nations that make up present-day Yugoslavia, created after the First World War, like the history of the Yugoslav movement, Yugoslav state and Yugoslav revolution, is one of turbulent events and complex social and political processes.

Before the First World War Serbia and Montenegro were kingdoms, Slovenia, Croatia, Bosnia, Herzegovina and Vojvodina were parts of the Austro-Hungarian state, while Macedonia and Kosovo, together with some parts of present-day Montenegro and Serbia, were under Turkey until the First Balkan War of 1912. Following the First World War —

The Golden Gate of Diocletian's Palace in Split, copperplate engraving from 1764.

started by the Austro-Hungarian attack on Serbia, using the 1914 Sarajevo assassination as a pretext — the Kingdom of Serbs, Croats and Slovenes, headed by the Serbian Karadjordjević family, was created by the Versailles Peace Treaty. This new state, with an area of 247,542 km², comprised the kingdoms of Serbia and Montenegro, which had extended their rule over Kosovo and Macedonia after defeating Turkey in the Balkan War, Croatia, Bosnia and Herzegovina, Slovenia and Vojvodina. The newly-formed kingdom, proclaimed on December 1, 1918, was a centralised state. Resistance to this form of unification and demands for a federal system were violently suppressed. The first government, composed of representatives of all the bourgeois political parties, summed up its programme with the slogan "Order and peace in the country". As early as December 30, 1920, it banned trade-union and other organisations under the influence of the Communist Party, which had been formed in Belgrade in April 1919 and was outlawed in August 1921. The vestiges of parliamentarianism were abolished by King Alexander I Karadjordjević on January 6, 1929, when he suspended the Constitution, dissolved political parties and imposed a monarcho-fascist dictatorship. At the end of the year, a royal decree changed the country's name to the Kingdom of Yugoslavia. After the assassination of King Alexander in Marseilles in 1934, a regency was established to act for his heir, still a minor, in which Prince Paul Karadjordjević played the major role.

Djerdap — Trajan's Tablet, lithograph by G. E. Herring from 1820.

The dictatorship was replaced by a limited form of parliamentarianism, but the nations and national minorities deprived of their basic rights gained nothing by this. The backward agrarian land, in which shepherds and farm workers made up three-quarters of the population, was among the least developed countries of Europe. The unsettled national question, coupled with social and other problems, led to the strengthening of a combined opposition, in which the Croatian Peasant Party was a leading force.

The Cvetković-Maček government, formed after the agreement between the Serbian and Croatian bourgeoisie giving Croatia a somewhat greater degree of autonomy, aligned itself with the Axis powers by signing the Tripartite Pact on March 25, 1941. On March 26 and 27, the people took to the streets in protest against this alliance. Following a military *coup*, the regency was abolished, the young king declared of age, and General Simović entrusted with forming a new government. Infuriated by this unexpected turn of events, which obliged him to delay his planned attack on the Soviet Union, Hitler and his allies attacked Yugoslavia without declaration of war on April 6. The war began with the heavy bombing of Belgrade on that date. About 50 German, Italian and Hungarian divisions invaded the country. The king and government fled abroad. After the country's swift occupation, the defeated kingdom was dismembered. The Third Reich annexed to itself the northern areas of Slovenia, while Italy took Ljubljana, the remaining south-western parts of Slovenia, parts of the Croatian Littoral, Dalmatia with the islands and the Gulf of Kotor. Bulgaria acquired the greater part of Macedonia, parts of Kosovo and south-east Serbia, and Hungary the regions of Bačka, Baranja, Medjimurje and Prekomurje. Part of Montenegro, Kosovo and Macedonia was ceded by Italy to Albania, which was under its protection. While the brief invasion was still in progress, the Axis powers organised the proclamation of the so-called Independent State of Croatia, which also incorporated Bosnia, Herzegovina and Srem, and installed the Ustashas led by Ante Pavelić in power. The Italians promised Montenegro to restore the Petrović dynasty. Hitler imposed a German occupation system on Belgrade and the remaining parts of Serbia, and formed a puppet administration under General Milan Nedić. The dismemberment of the country was accompanied by mass deportations and forced adoption of another religion, confiscation of property, confinement to concentration camps, mass slaughter, the "purging" of certain areas of Jews, Serbs and Gypsies, and the hunting down of communists.

After Josip Broz Tito had assumed its leadership in 1937, the Communist Party of Yugoslavia (CPY) had been consolidated and increased its activity and influence. At a meeting held on April 10, 1941, its Central Committee decided to call on the people to resist the occupiers. Its members and all freedom-loving people came forward as volunteers to defend the attacked country, but the ruling bourgeoisie was afraid to put arms in the hands of the workers and youth. The "April War" was too brief for the communists and

peoples of Yugoslavia to consider hostilities at an end. They could not reconcile themselves to the country's occupation and its division by rapacious neighbours.

The opening up of the Eastern Front with the German attack on the Soviet Union speeded up the decision to launch an armed uprising against the occupiers, which the Politburo of the Central Committee of the CPY passed at a meeting in Belgrade on July 4, 1941. The armed struggle flared up all over the country: in Serbia on July 7, in Montenegro on July 13, in Slovenia on July 22, in Bosnia-Herzegovina and Croatia on July 27, and in Macedonia on October 11. The fight began when the occupiers least expected it — three months after the invasion — and unforeseen by the rest of Europe, even those who welcomed it. It did not cease until May 15, 1945, although May 9 is celebrated as Victory Day. It was waged in towns and villages, on the plains, in the mountains and at sea, by day and by night. The people engaged in organised fighting based on guerrilla tactics and Partisan methods of warfare, liberating towns and districts. The first sizable regular army units, brigades, were formed from Partisan detachments on December 22, 1941. Yugoslavia became a theatre of war which the strategists of the lightning occupation had never anticipated. The liberation war of the Yugoslav peoples held down Axis forces numbering, on average, half a million fighting men, who could not be used on either the Eastern or Western Fronts from the middle of 1941 down to the capitulation of the Third Reich on May 9, 1945.

The Second Session of the Anti-fascist Council of National Liberation of Yugoslavia, held in the town of Jajce on November 29, 1943, laid the foundations of the future federal Yugoslav state as a community of equal peoples and nationalities. The Yugoslav National Liberation Committee was elected as the provisional government. This date is now celebrated as the national holiday, Republic Day. The liberation army henceforth began to receive military assistance from the Allies. Belgrade was liberated on October 20, 1944, with the help of units of the Red Army, on the basis of a previous agreement between the National Liberation Committee and the Soviet government. In the final operations, Istria, the Slovenian Littoral, and Trieste were freed by units of the Yugoslav army, which by then numbered 800,000.

Vraćevšnica Monastery, woodcut by an unknown artist from 1820.

In the four years of warfare against German, Italian, Bulgarian and Hungarian occupiers and quislings, 1,706,000 Yugoslavs lost their lives. The units of the Yugoslav army suffered around 305,000 dead and 425,000 wounded.

The Yugoslav Communist Party began the struggle for liberation and a more equitable social system under conditions of war in which the Yugoslav bourgeoisie had shown themselves more concerned with their own interests than those of the people and the country. Following the occupiers' orders, some had even played a part in the country's dismemberment. As the only organised force prepared to resist this, the communists declared war on the occupiers and those who served them. Their programme was succinctly expressed in the slogan: "Death to fascism — freedom for the people!" This historic declaration implied the liberation of Yugoslavia, but also a social system that differed from the one which had hastened the downfall of the anti-popular kingdom. The incitement of national hatred and religious fanaticism, and hence bloody conflicts, was countered by fostering brotherhood and unity, as a fundamental precondition for freeing the country from the occupiers and all the evils the occupation had brought its peoples.

The Yugoslav socialist revolution is a process of changing the manner of material production and thereby the circumstances in which political, social and intellectual life are shaped and function. Its moving forces, which appeared on the historical scene precisely in order to establish new social relations, are creating new values by their ability to perceive and eliminate their own mistakes. That is how these forces behaved in the reconstruction of the war-devastated country, in transforming it from an agrarian to an industrial state by strengthening the material base of socialist self-management. In the period from 1947 to 1982 gross material production (the GMP) increased about sevenfold, and production *per capita* fivefold. The GMP grew in this period at an average annual rate of 5.4 %. In 1985, its *per capita* average was in the region of 3,000 US dollars. The size of the population relying on farming for its livelihood dramatically declined — from 10.6 million in 1948 to 4.5 million in 1981. Between 1952 and 1983, 4.4 million pupils completed secondary schooling. From 1945 to 1983, 986,644 students graduated from universities and two-year colleges. Significant progress has been achieved in all scientific fields and in the arts, particularly among the nations which won their national emancipation in the liberation war. Institutions for science, the arts and education, and also modern information media have been organised and equipped in all republics and provinces. Large numbers of highly qualified personnel are contributing to the very intensive growth of material production and the development of all forms of intellectual and creative activity. Although the cultural emancipation of the working class and people cannot be measured only in terms of the number of institutions and qualified personnel, nevertheless the network of scientific and cultural institutions is a highly significant factor in the transformation of society. Judging by the quality of the achievements of its scientists, scholars and artists that have received international recognition, Yugoslavia can no longer be dismissed as a Balkan province. It has given to the world scientists and artists of the calibre of Tesla, Pupin, Milanković, Vuk Karadžić, Njegoš, Meštrović, Andrić, Krleža, Adamič, Baloković and Zinka Kunc-Milanov. No small number of Yugoslavs in the fields of the visual arts and cinematography, literature and music have won major international awards. An international reputation is enjoyed by a number of scientific gatherings and artistic events held in Yugoslavia: the Pula Film Festival, the Sterijino pozorje Theatre Festival in Novi Sad, the Dubrovnik Summer Festival, the Graphics Biennial in Ljubljana, the Ohrid Summer Festival, Struga Poetry Evenings, the Belgrade film, theatre and music festivals known respectively as FEST, BITEF and BEMUS, and the October Writers' Meeting in Belgrade, the Festival of the Child in Šibenik, and the symposium on socialism in the world held annually in Cavtat.

The national composition of the Yugoslav population demanded the policy and practice of national equality, the basis of the brotherhood and unity of the South Slav nations and nationalities (i.e. national minorities). There is no single official language, for every nation and nationality has the right to use and obtain education in the mother tongue. The largest number are speakers of Serbo-Croatian (in its Serbian and Croatian variants), then Macedonian, Slovenian, Albanian and Hungarian. Two scripts —Latin and Cyrillic — are in equal use. Besides the main religious communities —

Cover page of Petar Zrinjski's book "Mermaids of the Adriatic Sea" from 1660.

Serbian and Macedonian Orthodox, Roman Catholic and Islamic — there are others with a small number of adherents.

The first Constitution of the People's Republic of Yugoslavia was promulgated on January 31, 1946. It was possible to complete the task of drafting it in such a short time since the foundations of the federal system had been laid during the liberation war. Likewise, new forms of popular government had been devised and proved their worth functioning in wartime conditions. The necessity of reconstructing the war-torn country, the need to industrialise, the limited resources available and shortage of trained personnel demanded a centralisation of forces and means greater even than in wartime. Stalin's attack on the achievements of the Yugoslav revolution in 1948 caused the vanguard of the working class, and particularly its leaders, to take a more critical attitude towards the practice of the first socialist state, and towards the actions of its leaders. We succeeded in initiating the process of shattering the existing monopoly not only in the interpretation of Marxism but also in prescribing the directions and methods of developing socialism. All events in the international workers' movement since 1948 have confirmed that those who described this year as the beginning of the end of Stalinism were perfectly correct. It was of utmost importance for the course and outcome of our revolutionary process that we perceived the prospects, direction and method of developing the Yugoslav revolution and of realising the immediate and long-term interests of the working class. To this end, in 1950 a law was passed handing over the management of factories to the workers. Collectivisation of agriculture was abandoned: the land belongs to those who till it. Basic means of production are socially-owned, but anyone can work with privately-owned means.

The Programme of the League of Communists of Yugoslavia is based on an integral view of socialist self-management as a process for transforming a class-based society into an association of free producers. Its course has been marked by ascents and checks, but is bringing Yugoslav society steadily closer to the emancipation of labour and the individual — the goal of socialist self-management. This is the course we Yugoslavs call Tito's way, and which we have continued to follow since his death.

Our obligation to persist along this road is laid down in the 1974 Constitution. Its first article reads: "The Socialist Federal Republic of Yugoslavia is a federal state, being the state community of voluntarily united nations and their socialist republics, and of the socialist autonomous provinces of Vojvodina and Kosovo within the Socialist Republic of Serbia, based on the government and self-management of the working class and all working people, and a socialist self-managing democratic community of working people and other citizens and of equal nations and nationalities."

The federal state so defined is made up of the socialist republics of Bosnia-Herzegovina, Croatia, Macedonia, Montenegro, Slovenia and Serbia, and the two socialist autonomous provinces within the republic of Serbia. Unequal in size and population, the federal units have the same rights and duties in their common state, and are responsible for both their own development and the development of Yugoslavia as a whole.

The republics and provinces likewise differ in their level of economic development, the least advanced in this respect being Bosnia-Herzegovina, Montenegro, Macedonia and Kosovo. A federal fund and other forms of solidarity serve to promote the faster economic growth of these republics and Kosovo province. Encouragement is given to economic co-operation between the more and less advanced regions.

All joint state institutions and socio-political organisations in the Federation — the Yugoslav Presidency (i.e. presidential council), Federal Assembly and Federal Executive Council (Government) — are formed on the principle of parity. The Yugoslav Presidency comprises one member from each republic and province, elected in the assemblies of these federal units, and *ex officio*, the chairman of the Presidency of the Central Committee of the League of Communists of Yugoslavia. The Federal Assembly consists of the Federal Chamber and the Chamber of Republics and Provinces. The latter is made up of the same number of delegates from each of the republics and a certain number of delegates from both provinces. The Assembly proclaims the election of members of the Presidency, who are sworn in before it. The method of decision-making is based on these constitutional principles: "The working people, nations and nationalities make decision at federal level following the

Initial from the Divoš Gospels, a manuscript from the Bijelo Polje district, dating from before 1333.

1. *Triglav (2,863 m) in the Julian Alps in Slovenia, is the highest mountain in Yugoslavia. From an early age, every Slovene regards it as a matter of honour and prestige to scale this peak, so that expeditions to the top of Triglav are almost daily events. The whole Triglav area with its seven beautiful mountain lakes has been proclaimed a national park.*

2. *"Land of a Thousand Islands" is no more catch-phrase invented to attract tourists to Yugoslavia's fabulous coast. Scenes such as this one of the Korčula archipelago abound along the eastern Adriatic littoral, whose unspoilt natural beauty is carefully preserved.*

3. *Bosnia-Herzegovina, a land of mountains and forests, has always thrilled travellers with its spectacular landscapes, so different in the various seasons, and has inspired many to describe its wild beauty in poetry and prose.*

4. *The Gulf of Kotor (Boka Kotorska), the largest and most beautiful inlet of the sea on the Yugoslav Adriatic coast, is in the southern part, the Montenegrin Littoral. A series of submerged valleys cutting into the massifs of Lovćen (1,749 m) and Orjen (1,849 m), which rise steeply from its shores, the Gulf has a total coastline of 106 km.*

5. *The regions of Serbia offer great scenic variety, from rolling hills and grassy upland pastures to high forested mountains intersected by deep river gorges. Only a few areas have so far taken advantage of their natural beauty and other attractions to develop domestic and foreign tourism.*

5a. *The lowlands of Vojvodina, its fertile fields, intersected by canals and rivers, stretching away to the level horizon, present a serene and soothing picture. At sunset when the broad heavens are ablaze with colour, this spacious land has a restful beauty all its own.*

principles of consensus of the republics and autonomous provinces, solidarity and mutuality, equal participation of republics and autonomous provinces in the organs of the Federation in accordance with this Constitution, and the principle of responsibility of the republics and autonomous provinces for their own development and the development of the socialist community as a whole." It was these principles that guided us in editing this book, which aims to present Yugoslavia today.

This organisation of their common state originated from the struggle waged during the Second World War by all its nations and nationalities for their national and social emancipation, and from their determination to make Yugoslavia a community of equal and free people.

The processes of constituting social self-management as the basis of relations in society and of developing self-management-based democracy in a community of equal nations and nationalities were conditioned and made possible not only by the Yugoslav orientation and stands in regard to international relations, but also by this country's activities as an independent and non-aligned state in world affairs. Convinced that peaceful coexistence and active cooperation on an equal footing among states and nations is an essential condition for peace and social progress, Yugoslavia bases its foreign policy on the principles of respect of national sovereignty and equality, non-interference in the internal affairs of other countries, and the settlement of international disputes by peaceful means. In keeping with these principles, Yugoslavia remained outside blocs even in the troubled years of the cold war and the formation of military alliances, and was one of the initiators of the movement to bring together all those countries outside the military blocs. It was the host of the First Conference of Heads of State and Government of the Non-aligned States, held in Belgrade in 1961. At that time few statesmen and politicians expected this initiative to grow into the movement of non-aligned countries which would become a factor not to be ignored in world affairs. Abiding by the United Nations' Charter, Yugoslavia fulfils its international obligations and strives for all-round political, economic, scientific and cultural cooperation with other states and nations.

Our survey of Yugoslavia — which is better known

abroad for Tito and his endeavours in the field of international relations than for his contribution to its internal system — would not be complete if we did not quote Article 238 of the Constitution: "No one has the right to recognise or sign an act of capitulation, or to accept or recognise the occupation of the Socialist Federal Republic of Yugoslavia or any of its parts. No one has the right to prevent the citizens of the Socialist Federal Republic of Yugoslavia from fighting an enemy attacking the country. Such acts are anti-constitutional and punishable as treason. Betrayal of the country is the gravest crime against the nation and punishable as a serious criminal act."

By this the nations and nationalities of Yugoslavia show their awareness of the enormous sacrifices in human life made during the Second World War in the fight for national freedom and the country's independence, and their desire to develop social relations founded on the achievements of that struggle.

5b. *The magnificent massif of Mt. Šara (Šarplanina) is an area of towering peaks, forests, pastures and lakes offering splendid panoramas, such as this on the Kosovo side of the massif. In recent years, planned development has promoted tourism in this scenic area, with particular emphasis on winter sports, for which there are now several well-equipped centres.*

6. *Sheep rearing has a lengthy tradition in Macedonian, particularly in the Mavrovo, Galičnik and Lazaropolje areas. In the past, the shepherds of the Mijaci tribe would drive huge flocks from the uplands to winter in the areas bordering on Greece, and bring them back in the late spring. Neglected after the war, this important branch of livestock farming is now reviving.*

5 B

SLOVENIA

Slovenia, in the north-west of Yugoslavia, has an area of 20,251 km² and a population of 1,891,864 (1981 census): 1,712,445 Slovenes (90.6 %), 55,625 Croats (2.9 %), 42,182 Serbs (2.2 %), 26,263 persons who declared themselves Yugoslavs (1.4 %), 13,425 Moslems (0.7 %), 9,496 ethnic Hungarians (0.5 %), 2,187 ethnic Italians (0.1 %), and 30,241 other nationalities (1.6 %).

Slovenia's relief is highly diversified, with mountains, the karst plateau, river valleys and lowlands. The main mountain massifs are the Julian Alps with Mt. Triglav (2,864 m, the highest Yugoslav peak), the Karawankens (with several peaks over 2,000 m), the Kamnik Alps, Pohorje (1,543 m) and Snežnik (1,796 m).

In the heart of the Slovenian karst region, dotted with *polja* (depressions with arable land), sink-holes and about 10,000 subterranean caverns, lie the Postojna Caves, one of Yugoslavia's major tourist attractions. With their astonishing variety of stalagmites and stalactites, they rank among the most beautiful and largest caverns in the world. The remains of prehistoric bear, lion, hyena, wolf, deer and other creatures have been discovered here. The subterranean waters of

7. *Most of Slovenia is in the alpine region. Four of the ten highest peaks of Yugoslavia are in the Julian Alps and Karawankens. In the picture: a rack for drying hay typical of the Gorenjska region.*

8. *Between the massifs of the Savinja Alps, not far from the source of the river Savinja, lies the pleasant Logar valley, surrounded by forests.*

9. *Otočec Castle on an island in the river Krka, beside the Ljubljana—Zagreb highway, is one of the best preserved in Slovenia. Built in the 16th century, it has been adapted as a hotel but has retained its authentic atmosphere.*

10. *Lake Bled (2,130 m long, 1,032 m wide, 32 m deep) lies at an altitude of 501 m, north-west of Ljubljana, encircled by the peaks of the Julian Alps and Karawankens. The little church of St Mary of the Lake was built in the 15th century (and later renovated in baroque style) on a tiny island in the middle of the lake.*
In summer the water temperature reaches 24⁰ C, making it pleasant for bathing, while in winter the frozen surface is ideal for skating, curling and other winter sports. The lake is dominated by a medieval castle perched on a cliff (604 m).

Scene from daily life in 17th-century Slovenia, by Valvasor.

11.   *The famous Lipica Stud, dating back 400 years, lies in an oasis of greenery in the Karst area close to the Yugoslav-Italian border, 5.5 km from the town of Sežana. The beautiful white Lipizzanner horses, a mixture of local and Andalusian breeds, which are to be found all over the world, are ideal for dressage and as carriage horses. The stud runs an internationally renowned riding school.*

12.   *The pagan festival of "kurentovanje" is held every year in the second half of February. Wearing animal masks, the "kurenti" go around ringing bells in order to drive away winter and the evil spirits of nature. In the Ptuj area, and also in other parts of Slovenia, this ancient rite has grown into an exceptionally attractive event that draws many visitors.*

the Postojna Caves are the home of the unique "man fish" *(Proteus anguineus)*, found only in the caves of the Dinaric range.

The rivers of Slovenia mostly belong to the Danube (i. e. Black Sea) watershed. The Sava, the longest Yugoslav river, rises in Slovenia, where it is formed from two streams: the Sava Dolinka and Sava Bohinjka. The alpine region has a number of very lovely glacial lakes: Bled (1.5 km^2), Bohinj (4.5 km^2), and the seven Triglav lakes.

The Slovenian littoral is a narrow strip of land on the northern Adriatic with several tourist resorts on its indented coastline — Portorož, Piran, Izola and Koper.

The capital of Slovenia and largest city is Ljubljana. Other major towns are Maribor, Kranj, Celje, Novo mesto, Nova Gorica and Titovo Velenje.

From earliest times various cultures have met and intermingled on the territory of Slovenia. The most important aeneolithic sites are in the Ljubljansko Barje area. A considerable number of settlements from the 8th century BC have been discovered. The archaeological sites from around 500 BC at Stična and Vače (notable *situlae)* have yielded abundant remains of the iron-age Hallstatt culture. In the following centuries the region was inhabited by Illyro-Celtic

View of Ljubljana in the 17th century, by Valvasor.

tribes, conquered by the Romans towards the end of the 1st century BC. The latter built numerous fortifications and towns here, among them Aemona (on the site of Ljubljana), Neviodunum (Drnovo near Krško), Poetovio (Ptuj) and Celeia (Celje).

At the end of the 6th century, Slovenian tribes reached the western Alps and Adriatic Sea, and in the 7th century formed an early feudal state under Prince *(Knez)* Samo. After his death (658), these tribes, united in the principality of Karantania, remained independent until the mid-8th century, when Karantania was reduced to vassal status, first under the dukes of Bavaria and from 788 on under the Franks. Throughout the following centuries, and especially from the early 18th century on, Slovenian territory was subjected to the pressure of German feudal lords, attempts were made to Germanise the population, and the formerly free Slovenian peasants were deprived of their rights on the great feudal estates.

The desperately hard life of the peasantry led to several rebellions, the most significant of which were those in 1478 and 1515, when the Slovenian Peasant League was formed on an extensive area. Equally unsuccessful was the large-scale uprising in 1573, when the Slovenian and Croatian peasants joined forces against their feudal lords.

The peasant revolts and Reformation movement fostered the idea of Slovenian political and cultural affirmation. Primož Trubar (1508—1586) and other Slovenian writers of the Reformation period laid the foundations of the Slovenian literary language and literature. The first books in Slovenian were printed in 1550.

Under the influence of contemporary European movements, in the mid-19th century the Slovenian national programme was drawn up, calling for the unification of Slovenian lands, the demarcation of new internal borders based on the national principle within the Austro-Hungarian Empire, and the formation of Slovenia's own parliament and administration. This was a period of national awakening, the affirmation of the Slovenian language, the advancement of literature, an upsurge in the arts, and the creation of cultural and educational institutions. The most outstanding figures of this age were the writers France Prešeren (1800—1849) and Ivan Cankar (1876—1918).

13. *Predjamski Grad (the Castle before the Cave), not far from Postojna, was built in the 16th century at the entrance to a cave in a cliff 123 m above the mainly subterranean river Lokva. The coats-of-arms on it, from 1570, connect it with the robber baron Erazmus. It now houses a museum with exhibits from the neolithic period to the Middle Ages.*

14. *The small town of Trebnje, 50 km from Ljubljana, founded a colony for naive painters and sculptors of Slovenia, known as the Tabor, in 1971. The gallery in the town has a fine permanent collection of Yugoslav naive art. In the picture: sculpture exhibited in the area in front of the gallery.*

15. *Borl Castle, built in the 13th and renovated in the 17th century, stands on a bluff on the right bank of the river Drava, commanding a panoramic view of its surroundings — the Drava valley, Ptuj, Mt. Pohorje and the Slovenske Gorice hills.*

16. *Maribor (pop. 186,000), the second largest city in Slovenia, is an important industrial and communications centre with rich surroundings. As early as 1147 there is mention of a stronghold on what is now called Piramid hill. Notable among the old buildings is the 15th-century castle with a knights' hall and rococo staircase.*

17. *Šempeter — a Roman necropolis in the Savinja valley, 12 km from Celje. The tombstones from the 1st to late 3rd century are good examples of provincial Roman art.*

18, 19. *On a hill above the village of Hrastovlje, 12 km from Koper, stands a medieval church (12th—13th c.) in the old Istrian style. Its interior is decorated with frescoes (1409) by John (Ivan) of Kastav, including the remarkable Dance of Death. In the 16th century, the church was fortified with walls and towers.*

14

15

16

20. *Vače, the most famous iron-age site in Slovenia, lies on the western slopes of the Holy Mountain (Sveta planina), 34 km from Ljubljana. The rich finds from Vače have helped to give a more complete picture of the Hallstatt culture. The Vače situla (in the picture) is the finest work of art of the Hallstatt period found in Yugoslavia.*

21. *The church at Ptujska gora, a masterpiece of late Gothic architecture, built in the 15th century.*

22. *The baroque period left works of enduring value in Slovenia. The well-preserved religious and secular buildings attract the attention of visitors from this country and abroad.*

23. *The Virgin Mary and Child, in the church at Ptujska gora, is one of the finest late Gothic sculptures in Slovenia. This statue, like many others in the church, dates from c.1410.*

After one thousand years within the borders of foreign states, at the end of the First World War most of Slovenian territory became part of the newly-created Kingdom of Serbs, Croats and Slovenes (later renamed the Kingdom of Yugoslavia). But it was not until the national liberation war of 1941—1945 that the Slovenes finally attained full national and social rights.

In 1941, following the occupation of Yugoslavia, the Axis powers, having divided and annexed Slovenia, began a campaign to annihilate and assimilate the Slovenian nation. Under extremely unfavourable conditions — on a relatively small territory, intersected with communication lines and on the borders of Axis states, the Slovenes, organised in the Liberation Front, proffered armed resistance to the occupiers.

Ljubljana (pop. c. 305,000), the capital of the Republic of Slovenia, is a city with attractive squares and old buildings of architectural interest. Above the former Roman town of Aemona (remains of the Roman fortress in Jakopič Square), on the site of very ancient fortifications, rises the Renaissance castle, *Grad* (early 16th century). The square known as *Mestni trg* forms the centre of the charming old part of the city with its interesting buildings, mostly baroque. The finest arhitectural ensemble is Revolution Square *(Trg revolucije)* with the Ursuline church, building of the Philharmonium (founded in 1702) and modern cultural centre — *Cankarjev dom*. In addition to a university, Ljubljana has many other cultural and scientific institutions (theatres, an opera, the Academy of Sciences and Arts, etc.). The city organises many important events in the field of the arts, one of the most notable being the International Graphics Biennial.

Maribor, the main urban centre in north-east Slovenia, is the second largest city. Close to the Austrian border, it is connected by road with Ljubljana and Zagreb. There are many old buildings of interest, including the castle and town hall (both 15th century) and the cathedral, parts of which are from the 13th century. A city with a long industrial tradition, Maribor has a university, drama and opera companies and other cultural institutions.

Old fortresses of considerable interest include those of Škofja Loka in the Gorenjsko region and Ptuj in the Drava valley, with an eventful history stretching from Roman times, through the Middle Ages down to the recent liberation war. On a cliff above Lake Bled stands a picturesque castle probably built in 1004. Predjamski grad ("the castle before the cave") near Postojna, dating from the 16th century, is one of the most unusual medieval castles in Yugoslavia. Slovenia has over 15,000 buildings registered as cultural monuments.

About 51 % of the Slovenian population are economically active. Industrialisation and social transformation have greatly reduced the number of people engaged in agriculture (now below 9.4 % of the total population). Industry, mining, building, transport and tertiary activities employ 85 %, who create 90 % of the national income. Women make up 45 % of the working population. The *per capita* income is equal to that in countries which have attained a medium level of economic development.

The northern and central parts of Slovenia were soon caught up in the process of industrialisation in Central Europe. In the mid-19th century, a railway was built across Slovenia linking Central Europe with the Adriatic Sea.

Slovenia's natural resources include timber (more than half the republic is forested), non-ferrous minerals and

24. *Tromostovje ("Three Bridges") is the most attractive bridge in Ljubljana. The nearby Franciscan church, built from 1646 to 1660, has a fine altar and numerous frescoes. The Prešeren monument raised in 1905 is the work of sculptor Ivan Zajc. The poem "The Sailor" is carved on one side, and on the other a scene from the famous poet's epic "The Conversion at the Savica".*

25. *Portorož has grown in the past decade into a sizable holiday resort. In the picture: the Metropol, one of many hotels built on the Slovenian Littoral in recent years.*

26. *Narrow streets are a typical feature of small Istrian towns. In the picture: one such street in Koper.*

27. *Piran, a town older than Venice, was once a stronghold of pirates, from whom, according to legend, it takes its name. Today it is a popular seaside resort.*

28. *Novo Mesto on the river Krka is in the centre of the Dolenjska region of south-west Slovenia. Founded in 1356 and fortified in the 15th century, it is a noted centre of the pharmaceutical, textile and automobile industries. The main square with the Town Hall (early 18th c.), a fountain and arcades, the church of St Michael (Sveti Miklavž) with a painting by Tintoretto, and parts of the town walls have retained their original appearance.*

29. *Old handicrafts are still practised in many places. Some of their products, such as wickerwork goods, are in demand as souvenirs. In the picture: the market in Kranj with handicraft products on sale.*

View of Idrija in the 17th century, by Valvasor.

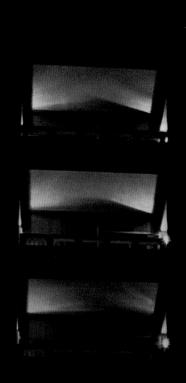

25

26

30

31

32

30. *Children feeding pigeons on a winter morning — a common scene in squares and parks and on riverside promenades.*

31. *Liberation Square in Ljubljana, dominated by the baroque Ursuline church from the early 18th century, with a plague monument raised between 1718 and 1726.*

32. *A dragon appears on the coat-of-arms of the city of Ljubljana, originally an Illyrian settlement, later the Roman city of Aemona. Carvings and sculptures of dragons can be seen in many places in the old part of the town.*

33. *Weeping willows beside Tromostovje, the triple bridge over the Ljubljanica in the old quarter of Ljubljana. Built in 1930 by the noted Slovenian architect Jože Plečnik (1882—1957), Tromostovje is a landmark in the old town.*

34. *View of Ljubljana, which has one of the best preserved baroque urban quarters in Yugoslavia, with the castle (Stari Grad), early 16th century, crowning the hill that rises above the city.*

various types of building materials. Power production is based on water power, coal and uranium. Arable land makes up 32 % of the total area. The condition for economic progress is research work and expansion of output in branches directed towards the home and foreign markets. The most expansive areas of the Slovenian economy are the production of electrical goods and household appliances, and the chemical, paper, metalworking, automotive and machine-tool industries. In addition to industry, crafts and agriculture, tourism is highly developed.

The textile, woodworking and food processing industries have long been important. Nine-tenths of total exports are from six industrial branches, in the first place the metalworking industry.

Slovenia's geographical position accounts for the heavy flow of traffic across its territory. The republic has a highly developed transport and communications network, which is constantly being further modernised. Koper, on the Slovenian littoral, is an important port for the transit of goods for Central Europe. There are three international airports: Ljubljana, Maribor and Portorož.

Particular attention is devoted to agriculture since the republic has relatively little fertile land. In the recent past, industrialisation and urban expansion have swallowed up considerable territory, so that regional plans now tend to

Žužemberk Castle, engraving by Valvasor, 17th century.

restrict non-agricultural activities to land unsuitable for farming. Half the arable land is used for growing grain crops, and one quarter for animal fodder. Considerable quantities of potatoes and other vegetables are raised.

Slovenia has many spas, mineral water springs with medicinal properties and climatic resorts, set in beautiful and tranquil surroundings. Among the most renowned are Rogaška Slatina, Dobrna, Čateške Toplice, Dolenjske Toplice and other places with hot springs.

On the northern coast of the Istrian peninsula lies Portorož ("port of roses"), the main seaside holiday and health resort. Close by, in the same bay, is the delightful old town of Piran. The economic hub of the Slovenian Littoral is Koper, which has an attractive centre of historical interest.

In the alpine region, much of which forms part of the Triglav National Park, there are four main areas. Most tourists flock to the Kranjska Gora winter sports centre, with the famous Planica ski-jump nearby. Bled is a popular holiday resort set on the lovely lake of the same name, and Lake Bohinj is renowned for the beauty of its surroundings. Further west, across the Triglav massif of the Julian Alps, lie the lovely valleys of the Soča and Trenta rivers and the little town of Bovec.

Traditional cottage industries and artistic handicrafts are still to be found in Slovenia: lace-making at Idrija, wrought-iron work at Kropa, various carved wooden products in the Dolenjska region, cut-glassware at Rogaška Slatina . . .

The Slovenian cuisine has a distinctive character of its own. Traditional folk customs that have survived are celebrated as regional festivities.

CROATIA

Of the six Yugoslav republics, Croatia is second largest in territory and population. It covers an area of 56,538 km², and at the time of the 1981 census had 4,601,469 inhabitants: 3,454,661 Croats (75.1 %), 531,502 Serbs (11.5 %), 379,057 persons who declared themselves Yugoslavs (8.2 %), and 236,249 others (5.2 %).

The republican capital is Zagreb with about 856,000 inhabitants. Other major cities are Split, Rijeka, Osijek, Pula and Dubrovnik.

In the north and north-east lies the Pannonian Plain — the spacious lowlands of Slavonia between the rivers Drava and Sava. In the north-west are the gentle hills of the Hrvatsko zagorje region; towards the south and south-west stretch the scenic regions of Banija, Kordun and Lika, the Dinaric Mountains and the extensive forests and rugged heights of Gorski kotar; along the Adriatic coast lie Istria, the Croatian Littoral (Hrvatsko primorje) and Dalmatia. Three distinct geographic regions come together here: the Pannonian, mountain and Mediterranean.

Geographic contrasts are reinforced by the different cultural and historical conditions under which the Croatian nation, proud of its homeland, its past and its present, lived and developed for more than a thousand years.

Remains of prehistoric man have been found in Croatia: the fossils of *Homo krapinensis*, of Neanderthal type, discovered in 1899 in a cave above the town of Krapina, not far from Zagreb.

Traces are also found of the Illyrians, whose king, Agron, ruled the territory from Šibenik in Yugoslavia to Lesh in Albania in the mid-3rd century BC. Soon after, Roman legions began their conquest and eventual occupation of the region. Several centuries of Roman rule left many monuments here (in Pula, Zadar, Solin, Split and elsewhere).

In the period of migration of Slav tribes in the early 7th century, the Croats reached the Adriatic coast. It was here and in the immediate hinterland that the history of Croatia and the organisation of the Croat state had their origins. The name of a Croatian prince (knez), Trpimir (845—864), is first mentioned in a deed of gift to a church in Split, in which he is referred to as *Dux Croatorum*. At the beginning of the following century, the Croatian king was Tomislav (910—928), followed by Petar IV Krešimir (1059—1074) and

35. *The Plitvice Lakes and their surroundings form a national park (19,200 hectares) with sixteen lakes connected by cascades and waterfalls, many caves and subterranean water courses. From the source of the river Korana, the lakes flow one into the next down to the lowest, Novakovića Brod, which pours over a waterfall, 30 m high, into the course of the Korana.*

36. *From the rugged heights of Mt. Velebit, the panorama stretches across the blue expanse of the Adriatic to the elongated island of Pag, running parallel with this massif. Velebit, like the entire Dinaric range above the Adriatic coast, is a barren, rocky limestone area with scant vegetation, sinkholes, polje and other karst features.*

37. *The Kornati, an archipelago of mostly uninhabited islands of exceptional beauty, not far from Zadar, attracts many trippers from the mainland and is a mecca of scuba-diving and fishing enthusiast.*

38. *The Opatija Riviera, at the head of the Kvarner Gulf, is one of Yugoslavia's leading tourist areas. Opatija itself has been a renowned holiday resort since 19th century, when it was often visited by royalty and the aristocracy of the Austro-Hungarian Empire.*

39. *Village houses in Slavonia, part of the Pannonian Plain, have long façades looking onto the courtyard. The side facing onto the street has small windows, from which the residents watch the world go by in their leisure hours.*

40. *Slavonia is noted for the breeding of strong horses that are the pride and joy of village households. Horse-drawn carts are not infrequently used when attending various feasts and celebrations, and even for work.*

41. *Many traditional customs and costumes have survived in Slavonia. This makes village weddings and other festivities very colourful occasions.*

42. *Besides the famous vineyards along the Adriatic coast, Croatia has noted wine-growing regions on the gentle hillsides sloping down to the Pannonian Plain. Large-scale vineyards have been planted in northern Croatia in recent years. In the picture: vineyards of the large Belje agricultural estate.*

43. *Pula, close to the southern tip of the Istrian peninsula, is the largest Istrian town. Mentioned in the legend of the Argonauts as Polan, it later became the centre of the Illyrian tribe, the Histri, which gave its name to the peninsula. Most remarkable of the monuments from the Roman period is the amphitheatre (arena) from the 1st century AD, still well preserved, which could hold 23,000 spectators.*

44. *The Brioni (Brijuni) are a group of islands off the south-west coast of Istria, not far from Pula. The largest, Veliki Brion, has remains of a late neolithic settlement. The entire island is an archaeologist's paradise, with notable remains from the Roman and Byzantine periods — a splendid Roman palace with terraces in Veriga bay, a huge complex of buildings known as the "Byzantine castrum" in Dobrika bay, and close by the ruins of an aisled Byzantine basilica from the 6th century. Veliki Brion together with the isle of Vanga was a summer residence of President Tito. They are now a national park.*

45. *The village of Solin beside the ruins of Salona, former capital of the Roman province of Dalmatia, is near the junction of roads leading to Split, Trogir and Sinj. The earliest known inhabitants of the area were the Delmatae tribe, which gave its name to Dalmatia. Later, ancient Greek colonists from the island of Vis built their settlement of Salona (4th—3rd c. BC), and from AD 78 it was held by the Romans. The town reached the peak of its prosperity during the reign of Emperor Diocletian (3rd—4th c.), who was born in Salona or its surroundings. In the picture: remains of Salona, about 10 km from Split.*

others down to 1102, when the territory lost its independence on entering into a union with Hungary.

From that time on, Croatian lands were under foreign rulers, mostly the Habsburgs. Some parts of the coast were for centuries part of the Venetian Republic, while certain areas were conquered by the Turks during their advance towards Central Europe. Throughout the centuries, the population often endured terrible sufferings as a result of oppression, warfare and their own struggles against alien rule. Testimony of this is the large number of medieval castles and fortifications.

The hard lives of the impoverished peasants, oppressed by their feudal lords, prompted them to rise in arms on several occasions. The most famous of these revolts is the great peasants' rebellion of 1573 led by the Croatian serf, Matija Gubec, which spread over north-west Croatia and into neighbouring Slovenia. Like the others, its was cruelly suppressed. In the 17th century, Croatian princes of the Zrinski and Frankopan families attempted to resist the growing hegemony of Vienna, but were captured and executed.

The first half of the 19th century was a period of national awakening and fierce resistance to the Germanisation and Magyarisation of Croatia (the Illyrian movement), led by members of the emergent Croatian bourgeosie. The "Illyrian renaissance" fostered awareness of the need to preserve the national identity and struggle against alien oppression.

Liberation from Austro-Hungarian rule came only at the end of the First World War, in 1918. Croatia became part of the newly founded Kingdom of Serbs, Croats and Slovenes (later renamed Yugoslavia), but the national question remained unresolved. The hopes and expectations of the Croats, and of other nations in the Kingdom of Yugoslavia, were not fulfilled during the twenty or so years of its existence.

In the Second World War, the Communist Party of Croatia, which did not recognise the dismemberment of the country or the fascist occupation, was the only organised force which aligned itself with the people, urging and organising active resistance to fascism from the beginning of the occupation, in 1941. Naval units of the People's Liberation

Army were formed in Croatia in 1942.

In the postwar period, Croatia made great advances. Its present level of economic development is above the Yugoslav average, with specialisation in the petroleum industry (oil fields in north-west Croatia, refineries in Rijeka, Sisak and Zagreb), ship-building (three large yards in Pula, Rijeka and Split) and the chemical industry. The major industrial centres are Zagreb, Rijeka, Split and Osijek.

The development of material culture on the territory of present-day Croatia began long before the arrival of the Slavs in these regions. Apart from palaeolithic finds and traces of Greek influence, there are many remains from Roman times, the most important of which are the amphitheatre in Pula and Diocletian's Palace in Split. The basilica of Bishop Euphasius in Poreč is the most outstanding of the monuments of Early Christian and Byzantine art.

Literacy among the Croats dates from the 9th century, when the Slavonic Glagolitic alphabet began to be used, in addition to the Latin, to spread the written word. The first texts in the Croatian language in the Latin alphabet appeared in the 14th century. In the 19th century, the Illyrian renaissance movement introduced a uniform literary language based on the *štokavski* dialect. Dubrovnik was the

46. *Veliki Tabor, a medieval castle in the Hrvatsko zagorje region, a picturesque hilly area noted for its vineyards, orchards and castles. In the Renaissance period it was renovated as a nobleman's palace, and has remained almost unchanged ever since.*

47. *The pilgrim church of St Mary of Jerusalem in the village of Trski Vrh, near Krapina, is a late 18th-century baroque structure surrounded by a rectangular wall (cincture). Its interior is richly decorated with rococo wall paintings.*

48. *Djakovo, an old town in Slavonia, south-west of Osijek, is best known for its impressive cathedral, raised in the second half of the 19th century by the celebrated Croatian bishop, patriot and art-collector, Josip Juraj Strossmayer.*

49. *Osijek (pop. c. 160,000), the main town of Slavonia, stands on the banks of the river Drava, 15 km upstream from its confluence with the Danube. It was the site of the Roman colony of Aelia Mursa, of the medieval citadel of Ezeck, and of the centre of a Turkish sanjak (administrative district), when it had a completely oriental appearance. It was here that Sultan Suleiman the Magnificent, during his advance on Vienna, built a pontoon bridge 8 km in length crossing the Drava and the Baranja marshes.*

50. *In the village of Kumrovec, birthplace of Josip Broz Tito, the Centre for Liberation War Veterans and Youth of Yugoslavia has recently been constructed.*

51. *Poreč, founded 25 centuries ago, is now the major tourist centre of Istria. Among art lovers it is best known for the basilica complex, a masterpiece of Early Christian art, built in the mid-6th century by Bishop Euphasius. It contains splendid wall mosaics comparable with those in Ravenna.*

View of Diocletian's Palace in Split (3rd—4th century), as reconstructed by E. Hebrard.

52. *Fishing, one of the main occupations of the coastal population from time immemorial, is still an important economic branch.*

53. *The Romanesque-Gothic cathedral of St Lawrence on the main square of the town of Trogir is famous for its richly carved main portal (1240), the finest example of Romanesque sculpture in Dalmatia. It takes its name, Radovan's portal, from the artist primarily responsible for it.*

54. *Trogir was founded on an islet between the coast and the larger isle of Čiovo in the 3rd century BC by Greek traders, who called it Tragurion (Isle of Goats). All that remains from this period is a Hellenistic relief of Kairos, god of the fleeting moment or opportunity.*

55. *Kastel-Gomilica, one of seven surviving fortified settlements, out of fourteen, strung out along a bay just north of Split. Originally intended for defence against the Turkish threat, the fortifications were raised in the 15th and 16th centuries. This fertile coastal strip is dominated by the bell-towers of these tiny places.*

56. *Donkeys are still a frequent sight in Dalmatia, being an irreplaceable beast of burden in this rugged region.*

57. *Susak, an island in the northern Adriatic, 11 sea miles from the larger island of Lošinj, has preserved a distinctive type of traditional women's costume. The inhabitants of the only settlement, also called Susak, isolated for centuries from their neighbours, have their own dialect and customs.*

58. *The costumes worn by the inhabitants of the narrow Adriatic coastal belt show the influence of the Dalmatian hinterland, but also of Venice and Turkey. In their colours and cut, the women's costumes derive from the early Renaissance period, with some baroque elements.*

"The First Agricultural Fair" in Zagreb in 1864, drawing from the exhibition catalogue.

most important centre in the periods of Renaissance-humanist and baroque literature. In modern times, Croatian writers have created a notable opus with distinctive national features that has achieved a place in European literature as a whole. Mention should be made of Miroslav Krleža (1893—1981), poet, novelist, playwright, essayist and encyclopaedist.

The Republic of Croatia has 125 museums, 720 libraries and 15 professional theatre companies. The institutions of higher education comprise 55 university faculties and 28 colleges, organised in four university centres: Zagreb, Rijeka, Split and Osijek. In addition, there are seven theological institutions for higher education.

Eight daily papers, over 30 weeklies, and 200 monthly magazines are published in Croatia. Radio Zagreb went on the air for the first time in 1926, and the Zagreb television station 30 years later. Today 60 radio stations and four television stations are in operation, the latter in Zagreb, Rijeka, Split and Osijek.

Zagreb is the capital and largest city of Croatia. Lying in the foothills of Mt. Medvednica, in recent years it has expanded across the river Sava with the construction of new

suburbs on its southern bank. The earliest recorded mention of the town is from the 11th century, when a bishopric was founded here. It originated from two urban settlements on neighbouring hills: Kaptol and Grič (Gradec). In 1242 both were overrun by the Tartars. In the same year, Bela IV issued a golden bull proclaiming Gradec a royal free city. In the mid-16th century, the city is first mentioned as the capital of Croatia and Slavonia. On the eve the Second World War, the Central Committee of the Communist Party of Yugoslavia had its headquarters in Zagreb, where Josip Broz Tito (born in nearby Kumrovec in 1892) spent many years as an active revolutionary and leading official of the illegal Party.

The first secondary school was opened in Zagreb in 1607, and an academy with lectures on philosophy, theology and law in 1669. From this Zagreb University developed, officially founded in 1874. Zagreb is the seat of the Yugoslav Academy of Sciences and Arts, the oldest institution of its kind in Yugoslavia, established in 1867. Other major scholarly and scientific institutions in Zagreb include the Miroslav Krleža Yugoslav Lexicographical Institute, the National and University Library, and the Ruđer Bošković Nuclear Institute.

Part of the old Upper Town (*Gornji grad*) has retained its original appearance. There are many buildings of historical and artistic interest, among them the neo-Gothic cathedral (originally founded in the 12th century) at Kaptol. The city has 24 museums and a large number of art galleries, the most famous being the Strossmayer Gallery, several theatres, newspapers and publishing houses, and radio and television stations.

On the south bank of the Sava stand the exhibition halls of the renowned Zagreb Grand Fair, the venue every year of major displays, of industrial and technical achievements, which attract exhibitors from all over the world.

Rijeka, at the head of the Kvarner Gulf, is Yugoslavia's biggest Adriatic port, notable in particular for its shipbuilding and maritime transport. Industrial installations are located close by on the bay of Bakar and the island of Krk, which has an international airport. Major Yugoslav shipping companies, whose vessels sail to all parts of the globe, have their headquarters in the city.

59. *View of Šibenik with its remarkable cathedral in the foreground. Juraj Dalmatinac (George of Dalmatia) was mainly responsible for its design and supervised its construction from 1431 until his death in 1473. A masterpiece in the mixed Gothic-Renaissance style, it was completed by another distinguished architect of the period, Nikola Firentinac (died 1505). Juraj himself carved the original and lifelike frieze of 74 heads on the outside of the cathedral apse — portraits of his contemporaries in Šibenik.*

60. *Hvar (299.7 km²), the sunniest Adriatic island, lies south of Split, beyond the island of Brač. Inhabited in the early neolithic age, it was settled in the 4th century BC by Greeks, from whose town, Pharos, it takes its name. In the southwestern part of the island, on the site of the Greek settlement of Dimos, stands the town of Hvar with several fine Renaissance bell-towers, a theatre from the early 17th century, picturesque fortifications above the town, Gothic and Renaissance mansions, a Renaissance town well (1529) and the cathedral of St Stephen in Renaissance and baroque style (16th—18th c.).*

61. *The city of Split, lying on a peninsula below Marijan hill, is in the very centre of Dalmatia. It grew up in the early Middle Ages within the walls of the vast palace built by Emperor Diocletian around AD 300 on the site of a former Illyro-Greek settlement named Aspalatos. Diocletian, a native of this area, intended this fortified palace covering 30,000 square metres as his residence after his retirement. When the nearby Roman city of Salona was destroyed by Avar and Slav tribes in the early 7th century, many of its inhabitants took refuge within the palace.*

62. *Dubrovnik, an autonomous city from the 12th century and a republic from the 15th, was famed for its shrewd merchants, skilful sailors and astute diplomats, who managed to preserve it from destruction and retain its independence right down to the early 19th century.*

64

66-A

66-B

63. *Entering the walled city of Dubrovnik through the western gate and over a stone bridge (1471), the visitor comes to the broad main street called Stradun. Strolling down it he passes Onofrio's Big Fountain (1438), the Renaissance church of the Holy Saviour (early 16th c.) and the Franciscan monastery (1499), and reaches Luža Square with Orlando's Pillar (1414), the Gothic-Renaissance Sponza Palace (1516—21) and the Rector's Palace (1431), seat of the Republic's government.*

64. *Zagreb has expanded since the Second World War across the river Sava, which was barely visible from the historic settlements of Gradec and Kaptol, the medieval nucleus of the city. The rapid growth of the population, from 57,690 in 1900 and 108,674 in 1921 to over 850,000 today, has necessitated the building of many new suburbs. In the picture: the Business Tower in Zagreb.*

65. *The neo-baroque Croatian National Theatre in Zagreb, built in 1895. In front of it stands the Well of Life (1905), one of the finest works by the celebrated Croatian sculptor, Ivan Meštrović.*

66. *View of the eastern side of the old part of Zagreb known now as Gornji grad (Upper Town). In 1242, when it was the fortified seat of a ban (governor), it was proclaimed a royal free city. On a nearby hill stood Kaptol, the seat of the archbishop, which developed parallel with Gradec. It was not until the mid-16th century that the name Zagreb was used for both settlements. The main square of Gradec is dominated by the 14th century Gothic church of St Mark. The baroque bell-tower was built between 1660 and 1725.*
On the preceding page: two scenes from modern Zagreb (66 A and B).

67. *The Stone Gate (13th c.) was the fortified entrance to the formerly walled medieval nucleus of Gornji grad. In the picture: the traditional festival of authentic folk music held every summer in Zagreb.*

Opatija, close to Rijeka, is one of Yugoslavia's leading tourist resorts, with a large number of hotels and excursion places.

Split, in the centre of the eastern Adriatic coast, is famous for its historical monuments, particularly the 3rd-century palace of the Roman emperor, Diocletian (included in UNESCO's register of the world cultural heritage). The imperial mausoleum, a temple, the vestibule, peristyle and gates are all well preserved. When the medieval town of Split grew up within the vast palace walls, some parts were put to other uses: the mausoleum became the cathedral and the Roman temple a baptistry. Certain chambers are now arranged for the holding of exhibitions and concerts. Close by Split, at Solin, are the extensive remains of the Roman city of Salona, which developed rapidly from AD 150 on and had some 50,000 inhabitants at the peak of its prosperity. Early Croatian historical monuments have also survived in this region.

Dubrovnik, on the southern Adriatic coast, is the best preserved Renaissance city in Yugoslavia (also included in UNESCO's register with a unique urban centre from the time of the Dubrovnik Republic. The site was already inhabited by the Romanised population when the Slavs settled here in the early 7th century. In the early Middle Ages it had the status of a commune and in the 14th century became a republic, famed for its merchant fleet. During its centuries of independence, the Dubrovnik Republic became a flourishing centre of trade and crafts, and attained a high level in the arts, literature and science. It was abolished following the Napoleonic conquest of the eastern Adriatic. Today Dubrovnik is the most famous tourist resort in Yugoslavia.

Osijek, the largest town of northern Croatia, stands on the site of the Roman colony of Mursa. *Varaždin,* in the north-west, is among the most attractive cities in the baroque style. These regions have many castles and palaces from the 15th to 19th centuries, of which Trakošćan Castle is the most picturesque.

Nine-tenths of the Yugoslav Adriatic coast, with almost one thousand islands, islets and large rocks, and innumerable bays, coves and headlands, lies within the Republic of Croatia. The largest peninsulas are Istria and Pelješac. The most populous of the 60 or so inhabited islands are Krk,

Lošinj, Rab, Brač, Hvar, and Korčula. The Kornati archipelago, Brioni islands (where Josip Broz Tito often stayed and had meetings with foreign statesmen), and the island of Mljet are national parks.

Croatia attracts about 50 % of domestic and 80 % of foreign tourists who holiday in Yugoslavia. International airports are located at Zagreb, Dubrovnik, Rijeka, Split, Pula, Zadar and Osijek. Pula, Rijeka, Šibenik, Zadar, Split and Dubrovnik are the major ports for tourist traffic. Many bays, ports and harbours have marinas for pleasure craft.

During the summer holiday season, many places stage arts and music festivals, the best known being the Dubrovnik and Split Summer Festivals and the National Film Festival in Pula.

Besides those mentioned, Croatia has several other national parks: Paklenica on Mt. Velebit, Risnjak in the Gorski kotar region, and the Plitvice Lakes, a unique natural phenomenon with sixteen lakes cascading into one another in a series of magnificent waterfalls (included in UNESCO's world heritage).

The broad Pannonian Plain, intersected by rivers, with its unusual flora and fauna, is an area noted for good hunting (game shooting) and fishing. The Kopački rit marshes are one of Europe's noted bird reserves.

Traditional customs, folk music, and festivities recalling various historical events have been preserved in many parts of Croatia. The *Sinjska alka* chivalric contest in Sinj, the *Moreška* mime dance on Korčula, Zagreb's annual international festival of authentic folk music, and numerous other traditional events are further attractions for tourists visiting Croatia.

BOSNIA-HERZEGOVINA

Bosnia-Herzegovina, which includes two large areas of Yugoslavia, is a unique cultural and socio-economic entity. Unforgettable in its diversity and scenic splendour, its territory, only 51,129 km² in area, combines the Orient and the West, Central Europe and the Mediterranean.

Bosnia-Herzegovina, central in position, occupies one fifth of Yugoslav territory. Not far from Sarajevo is the geographical centre of Yugoslavia. Of its 4,124,256 inhabitants (1981 census), 1,630,033 (39.5 %) are Moslem, 1,320,738 (32 %) Serbs, 758,140 (18.4 %) Croats, 326,316 (7.9 %) persons who declared themselves Yugoslavs, and 89,029 (2.2 %) people of other nationalities.

This republic abounds in striking scenic contrasts: high mountains, many rivers and streams and a number of lakes, but also fertile valleys and lowlands. Bosnia-Herzegovina has an exit to the Adriatic Sea (24 km of coast) around Neum. Perućica, the last virgin forest in Europe, forms part of the Sutjeska National Park, close to Foča. The Kozara National Park has one of the finest monuments to those who gave their lives in the National Liberation War.

Except for the Neretva, which flows into the Adriatic, the largest rivers — the Sana, Una, Bosna, Vrbas and Drina — belong to the Black Sea watershed. The Trebišnjica is Europe's longest subterranean river (rising again as the Dubrovačka river near Dubrovnik). There are a number of mountain lakes (on Treskavica, Zelengora), and several artificial lakes, of which the largest are Jablaničko on the river Neretva, Višegradsko on the Drina, and Bilećko on the Trebišnjica.

From ancient times various routes have led through Bosnia and Herzegovina and intersected on their territory. It was along these that conquerors came, endeavouring to leave their mark on the people and region by fire and sword, but also "travellers and merchants, builders and craftsmen, priests and wisemen, dervishes and poets, in short, people from all sides, led and impelled by the most diverse promptings, passions and interests" (Ivo Andrić).

Archaeological finds show that the region was inhabited in the old stone age (palaeolithic).

Many remains from the neolithic period indicate that Bosnia-Herzegovina was relatively densely populated at that time.

68. View of Mt. Prenj (2,155 m) in Herzegovina. Around this mountain, in a broad semi-circle, flows the river Neretva, beside which run the road and railway linking Sarajevo with Kardeljevo on the coast. On the northern side of Prenj, in the Neretva canyon, stretches the Jablaničko artificial lake supplying the Jablanica hydro-electric power plant.

69. Bosnia-Herzegovina is a predominantly mountainous land, but while the Bosnian highlands are mostly covered with dense coniferous and deciduous forests, much of Herzegovina is barren karst uplands with sparse vegetation. In the picture: livestock grazing on highland pastures.

70. Grain was formerly ground in watermills built on the abundant streams. Almost everywhere these have been replaced by steam-powered mills. In the picture: old watermills on the river Pliva near Jajce.

71. A typical Bosnian mountain village with steep-roofed cottages. On the small plots of arable land the main crops are maize, rye and barley, potatoes and cabbage. The harsh winter climate and hard life of villagers in such regions account for the steadily declining population, as more and more people move into towns.

72

73

75

74

73. *Islamic gravestones known as "nišani" are to be found scattered all over Bosnia-Herzegovina.*

74. *On Mrakovica, a peak of Mt. Kozara in western Bosnia, stands the monument to the people of the Kozara region who gave their lives in the National Liberation War (the work of sculptor Dušan Džamonja).*

In the latter half of 1942, this area was the scene of protracted and bitter fighting. A memorial complex has been raised to commemorate the Partisans who fell in battle here and the people of Kozara, described by the enemy as a "bulwark of the Partisan movement". In view of its natural beauty and historical associations, part of Kozara has been proclaimed a national park.

72—75. *A unique type of tombstone ("stećak") dating from the time of the medieval Bosnian state has been preserved in considerable numbers in Bosnia and Herzegovina. Mainly from the 14th and 15th centuries, they have the shape of a sarcophagus, house, slab or large stone cross, and are often carved with human and animal figures, birds, plants and various symbols. Some bear inscriptions and scenes of hunting, folk dancing and jousting. The best-known necropolis of these tombstones is at Radimlja, while one of the finest examples is from Donja Zgošća near Kakanj (now kept in the National Museum in Sarajevo).*

In the picture: detail from a "stećak" tombstone and the necropolis at Radimlja near Stolac, with 133 stones from the second half of the 15th century.

76. *The Kravica falls between Čapljina and Ljubuško in Herzegovina. Because of the porous limestone terrain, the water-level of the Kravica varies with the seasons.*

The Bosnian-Herzegovinian Rebellion, copperplate engraving by Vierge, 19th century.

From AD 230 on, the Romans began their penetration of this territory, which they held until the 5th century AD, leaving behind significant traces of their culture.

After the fall of the Western Roman Empire (AD 476), it frequently changed hands until it came under the rule of Byzantium, where it remained until the arrival of the Slavs in the early 7th century.

The name *Bosna* is first mentioned in the 10th-century writings of the Byzantine emperor, Constantine Porphyrogenitus. In the Chronicle of Father Dukljanin it is described as a spacious land, and as early as 960 as an independent region on an equal footing with Raška (Serbia) and Croatia.

The land of Hum or Zahumlje, later Herzegovina, developed parallel with Bosnia in the early Middle Ages.

In the reign of the Bosnian *ban*, Kulin (1180), Bosnia was a relatively well-organised state.

The first reliable evidence of the appearance of the Bogumil (Patarene) faith dates from 1199. With the organisation of the Bosnian Church, this became the official religion. From its first appearance, as a form of resistance to the Catholic Church, until the downfall of the Bosnian state (1463), the Pope treated Bosnia as an heretical land, sending crusades against it. Bogumilism spread very rapidly through

Bosnia and Zahumlje, since it here renounced one of its fundamental principles — resistance to feudalism. This facilitated the cooperation of the state and the Bosnian Church, which for its part, unlike the Catholic and Orthodox Churches, made no attempt to become a major landowner.

The Bosnian state reached its zenith under Tvrtko I Kotromanić (1358—1391), who in 1377 was crowned "king of Serbia, Bosnia, the Coast and Western Regions", and in 1390 was known as "king of Raška, Bosnia, Dalmatia, Croatia and the Littoral". It was in this period that the Turks began their incursions into Bosnia.

After the death of King Tvrtko, Bosnia was torn by religious disputes among the leading feudal lords. In particular, the struggle against Bogumilism was intensified, the Pope demanding that it should be rooted out "by the sword, fire and death".

A notable feature of Bogumilism in Bosnia-Herzegovina was the raising of an unusual type of tombstone (stećak), usually in the shape of a sarcophagus, carved with mysterious symbols and also scenes of contemporary life. More than 58,000 of these are scattered over the region.

The Ottoman Empire conquered Bosnia in a swift campaign in 1463. With the fall of the town of Jajce and the death of the last Bosnian king, Stjepan Tomašević, the medieval Bosnian state ceased to exist. In 1482 Herzegovina was conquered.

Ottoman rule brought with it the specific Turkish feudal system and the penetration of oriental-Islamic civilisation, accompanied by widescale conversion to Islam. Although there is no direct evidence in historical sources that the majority of Bogumils were immediately converted, this supposition appears probable, since the Turks arrived when persecution of the "hateful Manichean heresy" was continuing unabated, and the Bogumils are known to have had connections with the Turks even before the occupation.

Throughout the period of Turkish rule over Bosnia and Herzegovina, the local population was subjected to persecution and forced conversion to Islam. This gave rise in the 17th, and particularly the 18th century to growing resistance, rebellions and uprisings. Agrarian exploitation resulted in frequent peasant revolts in Bosnia and Herzegovina in the 19th century too. The largest in scale were those from 1875 to

77. *The Buna Spring (Vrelo Bune), not far from Mostar, is a famous beauty spot where the short river Buna, a tributary of the Neretva gushes forth from a cave below a sheer cliff, beside which stands a dervish tekke (monastery) from the early 17th century. Nearby is the village of Buna, and in the vicinity, also on the left bank of the Neretva, the Orthodox monastery of Žitomislići. Its church, founded in the 15th century, was rebuilt in 1585.*

78. *Gradačac is a small town noted for its historical monuments, including the clock-tower raised by Husein-Kapetan Gradaščević, known as the "Dragon of Bosnia", who led an army of Bosnian rebels against the forces of the Porte in 1831.*

79. *The royal citadel of Vrandak in the gorge of the river Bosna, north of Zenica, is first mentioned in the 15th century, and was for some periods the seat of Bosnian rulers. Above the village of Vrandak stand the ruins of this mighty medieval fortress, which held back many would-be conquerors in its time.*

80. *Travnik, an attractive town below Mt. Vlašić, on the river Lašva (in which Illyrians, Celts and Romans panned for gold), was for two centuries the administrative centre of the Bosnian pashalik. Over the past three decades, a new town, Novi Travnik, has been built close by, while the old town preserves the authentic atmosphere of bygone times.*
Travnik was the birthplace of Ivo Andrić, winner of the Nobel Prize for Literature in 1961, whose house is now a commemorative museum. Andrić's famous novel "Bosnian Story" (Travnička hronika) vividly describes life in the town when the Travnik viziers and foreign consuls lived here. In the picture: Travnik Castle.

81. *Bihać, a town on the river Una, first mentioned in 1260, has a number of interesting old buildings, notably the Fetija mosque, formerly a Gothic church, and the fortress from the Turkish period, now in ruins.*

The First Session of the Anti-fascist Council of National Liberation of Yugoslavia (AVNOJ) was held in Bihać on November 26/27, 1942.

In the picture: the ruins of Sokolac Fortress above Bihać.

82. *In 1945 Bosnia-Herzegovina had a total of 30 km of asphalt road, compared with over 8,000 km of modern roads today.*

83. *View of Počitelj, an old town above the left bank of the river Neretva in Herzegovina. In the Middle Ages it was an important stronghold controlling the Neretva valley as far as the sea. The remains of the old castle from the time of the medieval Bosnian-Herzegovinian state and the Turkish period are perched like an eyrie on top of the hill. Town walls and towers enclose the houses, mosque (1563), madrasah (Islamic religious school, 1664) and baths. Now restored, Počitelj attracts many tourists and artists.*

84. *Banjaluka, the second largest town in Bosnia-Herzegovina, is notable for its abundant greenery, cultural monuments, ancient fortress and new buildings raised after the 1969 earthquake.*

1878, with a pronounced anti-feudal and national liberation character.

Turkey's failure to suppress the uprising did not, however, benefit the insurgents but Austria. Aided by Germany, it engaged in intensive diplomatic activity to attain its imperialist aspirations towards Bosnia and Herzegovina. By a decision of the Congress of Berlin in 1878, Austria-Hungary was entrusted with the administration of these territories.

Aiming to secure its position in the Balkan peninsula and crush the liberation movement in Bosnia and Herzegovina, Austria-Hungary subsequently declared their annexation. Class conflicts were exacerbated in this period. With the development of crafts and industry, a working class began to emerge.

National liberation movements and the idea of South Slav unity gained growing support in Bosnia and Herzegovina. The assassination of Archduke Franz Ferdinand, heir to the Austro-Hungarian throne, in Sarajevo in 1914 by a member of the Young Bosnia organisation was used by Austria-Hungary as a pretext for attacking Serbia, thus triggering off the First World War.

In the Kingdom of Yugoslavia, none of the vital problems of the peoples of Bosnia and Herzegovina were resolved. Deprived of national rights, this backward agrarian land, whose mineral wealth and timber were exploited in equal measure by foreign capital and the home bourgeoisie,

Jajce, copperplate engraving by J. Harrewy, 18th century.

was one of the most underdeveloped areas of Europe: almost 80 % of the population were illiterate, and average life expectancy was scarcely 38 years.

Some of the major events of the Yugoslav Liberation War took place in Bosnia-Herzegovina: the first regular unit of the Liberation Army was formed in the small town of Rudo; crucial battles were fought on the rivers Neretva (the battle for the wounded) and Sutjeska (when the supreme commander, Tito, was wounded); the Anti-Fascist Council of National Liberation of Yugoslavia was founded in Bihać in 1942, and at its second meeting in Jajce (November 29, 1943) laid the foundations of the present Yugoslav state — the Socialist Federal Republic of Yugoslavia.

As one of the Yugoslav republics, Bosnia-Herzegovina has made great socio-economic progress: much new industry has been built (in relation to 1939, twenty times the amount), transport and communications have been developed, agriculture has improved, widespread changes have occurred in the conditions and way of life in both town and country, and striking advances have been achieved in education, science and culture.

Before the Second World War there was not a single institution for higher education in Bosnia-Herzegovina. Today there are four universities (Sarajevo, Banjaluka, Tuzla and Mostar), which graduate over 7,000 students annually. From 1948 up to the end of 1984, 123,000 students had graduated from the university faculties and colleges (a total of 41 higher education institutions).

The republic has its own Academy of Sciences and Arts and a large number of scientific research institutes.

Sarajevo (pop. 449,000) is the capital of Bosnia-Herzegovina and the most developed economic, communications (railway, highways, international airport) and cultural centre in this republic. Parts of it are a living museum, crowded with buildings of cultural and historical interest: the Bey's mosque, the most imposing Islamic place of worship in the Balkans; Ali-pasha's mosque, an exceptionally attractive work of oriental architecture; and the Kuršumli madrasah (theological school), the oldest educational institution in these regions. Other notable buildings include the Jewish synagogue, the Orthodox church of SS Michael and Gabriel, the Haji-Sinan tekke (monastery)... The most attractive

85. *Jajce, once the capital of medieval Bosnian rulers, stands above the Pliva waterfalls, close to where the river flows into the Vrbas. There is much here to recall the town's long history: catacombs, the fortress, St Luke's tower, mosques, a Mithraic temple, and some other Roman remains.*

The Second Session of the Antifascist Council of National Liberation of Yugoslavia (AVNOJ), at which the foundations of the present Yugoslav state were laid, was held in Jajce on November 29/30, 1943.

In the picture: panorama of Jajce with the Pliva falls.

86. *Courtyard of a Moslem house in Mostar with oriental architectural features in its lay-out and decoration.*

87. *Mostar, a town on the clear green river Neretva, draws many visitors with its attractive appearance and many interesting oriental-style buildings, dating back to the 15th and 16th centuries. The famous bridge ("most"), built in 1566, from which the town takes its name, spans the swift-flowing river with a single arch, 30 m long.*

88. *Višegrad, in Turkish times an important caravan station on the road from Dubrovnik to Istanbul, has become famous through its bridge over the Drina, an outstanding achievement of Islamic architecture. It was constructed in 1577 by the celebrated Turkish architect Mimar Sinan, on the order of Grand Vizier Mehmed-pasha Sokolović.*

89. *Neum, on the short stretch of the Adriatic coast belonging to Bosnia-Herzegovina, has grown into a popular seaside resort thanks to the construction of modern hotels, and is now attracting more foreign as well as Yugoslav holidaymakers.*

88

89

94

95

90. *The Gazi Husrev-beg mosque (and madrasah) in Sarajevo. One of the largest Islamic religious buildings in the Balkans, it was constructed in the Early Istanbul architectural style, being completed in 1530. The square central area (13 × 13 m) is surmounted by the main dome, 26 m high.*

91. *Panorama of Sarajevo, capital of Bosnia-Herzegovina, founded (before 1463) by the Turks, who called it Sarai. In the 16th and 17th centuries it ranked among the leading centres of trade in the ,Balkans. The old quarter of the city with its market district and many outstanding oriental buildings has retained much of its original appearance. Besides its many mosques, Sarajevo has Orthodox and Catholic churches and a synagogue.*

92. *With its oriental atmosphere and numerous monuments of Islamic art and culture, Sarajevo is particularly interesting for foreign visitors. Their number has considerably increased since the holding of the 1984 Winter Olympics here.*

93. *Baščaršija, the old market district of Sarajevo, is a "must" for all visitors to the city. In the many small craft shops, where tourists can purchase fine handicraft products as souvenirs, lively bargaining is an essential part of the transaction.*

94. *The ceremonial opening of the XIV Winter Olympic Games in Sarajevo in 1984. The organisation of this large-scale event, which received general praise, showed that Yugoslav experts are eminently capable of staging such international competitions.*

95. *Mt. Bjelašnica (2,067 m) was the venue of the men's slalom and grand slalom contests. Its excellent ski slopes have two- and three-seater gondolas and three ski lifts. The Famos Hotel at Babin Dol is 31 km from Sarajevo.*

Battle of Bosanska Gradiška, copperplate engraving from 1789.

part of Sarajevo is the Baščaršija quarter with many its multitude of craft shops and old oriental-style buildings.

A unique combination of big city, cultural and historical monuments and winter sports centre, Sarajevo hosted the XIV Winter Olympic Games in 1984.

Banjaluka, the second largest town in Bosnia-Herzegovina, is noted for its parks and abundant greenery and its numerous cultural-historical monuments. Outstanding among them are the large fortress, the Kaštel, its walls washed by the river Vrbas, the Ferhadi and Arnaudi mosques with slender minarets (16th century), the Trappist monastery, the monastery church of Gomionica and the church at Petrićevac.

Banjaluka suffered severe earthquakes in 1969 and 1981, but has been restored thanks to aid from all parts of Yugoslavia.

Mostar, the biggest city in Herzegovina, is a place that has evoked the admiration of many writers and travellers.

"Mostar, it is well known, is one of the loveliest and most unusual towns that man has built in this part of the world. In the canyon of a river, with its wonderful bridge, stands this distinctive urban structure, woven from stone and sun, greenery and water" (Ivo Andrić).

Tuzla and its surroundings are industrial in character. Its salt deposits were exploited by the ancient Greeks (the river Jala which flows through Tuzla takes its name from the Greek word *jalos*=salt), and then by the Romans. Today the huge salt deposits provide the basis for a highly-developed chemical industry. The Tuzla basin is rich in brown coal and lignite.

While the old Bosnian castles and strongholds, which number about 400, were raised in river gorges, on steep hillsides, on mountain peaks, or at crossroads, so that the kings, bans and feudal lords could ensure their safety, modern urban settlements are designed to meet the needs of contemporary man. The rapid growth of towns has contributed much to raising Bosnia-Herzegovina from the status of a "backwater province".

SERBIA

Serbia, which includes the autonomous provinces of Vojvodina and Kosovo, covers an area of 88,361 km², one third of the territory of Yugoslavia. At the time of the 1981 census, it had 9,313,675 inhabitants: 6,182,155 Serbs (66.4 %), 1,303,034 ethnic Albanians (14 %), 390,468 ethnic Hungarians (4.2 %), 215,166 Moslems (2.3 %), 149,368 Croats (1.6 %), 147,466 Montenegrins (1.6 %), 441,941 persons who declared themselves Yugoslavs (4.7 %), and 484,078 persons of other nationalities (5.2 %).

This republic occupies the eastern part of Yugoslavia, and apart from the Pannonian Plain in the north, is mostly hilly and mountainous terrain, intersected by extensive fertile depressions and many river valleys. The highest mountains are Kopaonik (which suffered a series of earthquakes in the early 1980s, the damage from which has been repaired with help from the whole of Yugoslavia), Tara, Zlatibor, Zlatar, Šara and Prokletije. The Danube, Drina, Lim, Vlasina and some other rivers have been dammed to create artificial lakes that have become tourist, recreation and sports centres. The rivers ultimately flow into three seas: the Adriatic, Black and Aegean.

The history of the peoples living on this territory has always been turbulent. Lepenski Vir (an archaeological site in the Djerdap Gorge of the Danube) was permanently settled as early as the 6th millennium BC. Important neolithic sites include Starčevo near Pančevo (5th millennium BC) and Vinča near Belgrade (4000—3000 BC), which have given their names to prehistoric cultures.

Later inhabitants were the Celts, Thracians, Illyrians, Greeks and Romans.

The area was crossed by exceptionally important routes which linked different worlds and cultures. One of these followed the Dunabe through the Djerdap Gorge (Iron Gates). At the end of the 1st century AD, the Roman emperor, Trajan, built a bridge over the Dunabe at Kladovo (1,500 m long and supported by twenty piers), which was one of the wonders of the world at that time. Another route linked the Western and Eastern Roman Empires. A number of major cities grew up along or near this route: Sirmium (present-day Sremska Mitrovica) — a metropolis of the Roman Empire in the 3rd and 4th centuries, Singidunum (Belgrade), Naissus (Niš) — birthplace of Constantine the

96. *The Djerdap Gorge (Iron Gates) of the Danube is the largest river gorge in Europe. The damming of the river near Kladovo has turned this formerly treacherous section into an elongated lake supplying water for the giant Djerdap hydro-electric plant. The settlement of a previously unknown European culture of the 6th millennium BC was discoverd at nearby Lepenski Vir in 1965.*

97. *Serbia still has extensive areas of unspoilt natural beauty. One of these is the surroundings of Vlasinsko Lake, where only the gentle hum of pleasure craft and the tinkle of sheep-bells break the profound silence of this tranquil spot.*

98. *Remains of formerly mighty fortresses can be seen along the banks of the Danube. The largest and best preserved of these is Smederevo (built between 1428 and 1430), and the most picturesque, Golubac Castle, not far from Veliko Gradište, whose tall towers remind the traveller that time passes as quickly and inexorably as the waters of the river. In the picture: Golubac Castle (14th c.)*

99. *The grassy slopes of Serbia's hills provide plentiful livestock fodder, but the mower must have both skill and stamina for this back-breaking task. Traditional mowing contests are held in various parts of the republic, one of the most interesting being at Rajac, south-west of Belgrade.*

100. *Modern roads now cross wild regions until recently almost inaccessible. One of these, the main road from Niš to the Bulgarian frontier, tunnels through rock as it follows the Sićevo gorge.*

101. *Maglić Castle, perched on a steep hill above the river Ibar, was probably built in the 14th century. Long abandoned, it is now merely a picturesque sight for travellers along the Ibar highway.*

102. *Kopaonik, a mountain justly named the "beauty of Serbia", has been rapidly developed as one of Yugoslavia's leading ski resorts in recent years. Its modern hotels, network of ski-lifts and ideal slopes meet the requirements of even the most demanding foreign and Yugoslav winter sports enthusiasts.*

Great, Romuliana (Gamzigrad, near Zaječar), Iustiniana Prima (Caričin grad near Lebane), Ulpiana (near Priština) and others.

The South Slavs arrived in the Balkans in the 6th and 7th centuries, the Serbian tribes settling in the areas around the rivers Drina, Zeta, Piva, Tara, Ibar and Morava. In the 12th century, the regions of Raška and Zeta were united in an independent Serbian state under Grand Prince *(veliki župan)* Stefan Nemanja, who ruled from 1170 to 1196. (The centre of the first Serbian state, the old citadel of Ras, and the nearby monastery of Sopoćani are included in UNESCO's register of the world cultural heritage.) Medieval Serbia attained the peak of its development and might in the reign of Stefan Dušan (king from 1331, emperor from 1346 to 1355). Nemanja's son, Sava, succeeding in gaining recognition for the independent Serbian Orthodox Church in 1219.

The strengthening of the Nemanjić state and Church was accompanied by the flowering of the arts and culture. There was intensive translation and manuscript-copying activity, and original Serbian literature first appeared with the writing of royal biographies. The surviving churches and monasteries, mostly royal foundations, painted with frescoes and adorned with icons, testify to the high quality of architecture and painting in the medieval Serbian state. Art historians divide this art into two stylistic epochs: the Raška style — Studenica (late 12th c.), Žiča (early 13th c.), Mileševa (13th c.), Sopoćani (13th c.), the Patriarchate of Peć (12th—14th c.), Holy Archangels (14th c.), Gradac (13th c.), Arilje (13th c.), Dečani (14th c.); and the Serbo-Byzantine style — St Mary Leviška (early 14th c.) in Prizren, and Gračanica (14th c.). Architectural sculpture followed the development of architecture. The wall painting was influenced by the Byzantine tradition.

The powerful state, level of economic relations, the class structure of society and the multitude of social links and relationships led to the appearance of Dušan's Code (approved by assemblies in 1349 and 1354), a celebrated medieval legal document.

After the battle of Kosovo in 1389, Serbian lands became vassal territories of the Turks, whose incursions reduced the Serbian state to its former northern regions, towards the rivers Danube and Sava. For the next seventy years, this state, whose rulers now held the title of despot instead of king, managed to resist Turkish pressure and retain its independence. At this time Belgrade first became the Serbian capital (1403). The last stronghold, Smederevo on the Dunabe, fell to the Turks in 1459. Having lost its independence, Serbia was subjected to harsh Turkish rule for several centuries.

The architectural monuments raised after the battle of Kosovo belong to the Morava style — buildings with trefoil ground-plans and low-relief ornamentation, decorated with colourful frescoes: Lazarica (14th c.), Gornjak (15th c.), Ljubostinja (15th c.), Kalenić (15th c.), Ravanica (15th c.) and Resava (15th c.). This was a period of considerable literary and translation activity.

In the centuries of Turkish rule, the people withdrew to the wooded hills and upland pastures, engaging primarily in livestock farming. Monasteries became the centres of religious life and preserved the cultural and national traditions of the Serbian people.

To escape Turkish oppression, many fled from their ancestral hearths. From Kosovo and Metohija there were two large-scale migrations northward to the Pannonian Plain.

During the lengthy period of Ottoman rule, the Serbs resisted conversion to Islam and loss of their national character, raising rebellions and taking to the woods as outlaws (hajduks). The first major national uprising broke out at Orašac in the Šumadija region in 1804, under the leadership of Karadjordje. This was both a revolt against Turkish cruelty and a struggle to regain national independence and throw off the feudal system. Although suppressed in 1813, the liberation and anti-feudal aspirations burst forth again only two years later in the second Serbian uprising, which ended with the recognition of Serbian autonomy (1830). After the Russo-Turkish War of 1876—1878, in which Serbia took part, its complete independence was recognised at the Congress of Berlin (1878). Several years later, the principality was proclaimed a kingdom.

The foundation of the High School (1863) marked the beginnings of higher education in Serbia. It was followed by the establishment of a number of other important cultural institutions — the National Library, National Museum,

103. *The remains of the late Roman fortress of Romuliana at Gamzigrad, near Zaječar, comprise walls, gates and parts of towers from the 3rd and 4th centuries. The floor mosaics excavated here are among the finest found on the territory of Yugoslavia.*

104. *Studenica, one of the most famous Serbian monasteries, stands in a secluded spot not far from the village of Ušće on the Ibar highway. All three monastery churches have retained their original appearance: the church of the Virgin Mary from the late 12th century, the small church of St Nicholas from the late 13th, and King's church from the early 14th century. The frescoes in the oldest church have the earliest inscriptions in the Serbian language found on wall paintings.*

105. *Žiča monastery near Kraljevo, founded by King Stephen the First Crowned (Stefan Prvovenčani, 1220—1227), was the first seat of the Serbian archbishopric. Its frescoes date from the 13th and 14th centuries.*

106. *Sopoćani monastery is a treasure-house of frescoes considered to rank among the finest European paintings of the 13th century. Created when Byzantine fresco painting was at its zenith, they have often been compared by art historians with the work of Giotto.*

107. *The powerful Sopoćani frescoes have represented the achievements of medieval Serbian art at numerous exhibitions abroad. In the picture: detail from the fresco of Christ's Nativity.*

108. *"I, the sinful deacon Gregory, unworthy to be called deacon, have ornamented with gold this Gospel of the glorious Prince Miroslav, son of Zavida," runs an inscription on the Miroslav Gospel, the oldest extant Serbian codex, dating from the 12th century.*

109. *The frescoes of Mileševa monastery near Prijepolje, a foundation of King Vladislav, are among the outstanding works of European painting in the first half of the 13th century. With its refined use of colour and nobility of expression, the White Angel (Angel at Christ's Sepulchre) is considered one of the finest.*

110. *Once a year Orthodox monasteries and churches celebrate the feast-day of their patron saint, an occasion which has traditionally been a popular festivity, when the local people gather and make merry in the spacious churchyards. In the picture: festivities in front of Mileševa church (13th c.) near Prijepolje.*

111. *Ljubičevo Stud Farm near Požarevac, founded in 1860, has played an important role in horse-breeding in this part of Serbia. The Ljubičevo Horse Show, held annually in Požarevac, with a variety of equestrian contests, always draws large crowds.*

112. *Trumpet bands are often a feature of village fairs and gatherings. Guča, in western Serbia, is famous for its annual fair at which many bands compete in displaying their skill on the old Serbian military trumpet. This colourful and clamorous event has become a great tourist attraction.*

113. *Stevan Filipović, a young Partisan captured by the occupation forces, was publicly hanged in the town of Valjevo in 1942. Beneath the gallows, this courageous young worker, with upraised arms called on the people to continue their resistance. A monument to the Partisans and people of this region who fell in the liberation war, with the figure of Stevan Filipović (the work of the Zagreb sculptor Vojin Bakić) was raised at Valjevo in 1960.*

National Theatre (1869), the Serbian Learned Society, later the Academy of Science (1864), the State Printing Works, and official gazette (*Novine serbske*). The 19th century produced some outstanding cultural figures, in the first place Vuk Stefanović Karadžić (1787—1864), a self-taught peasant lad who became a scholar of international renown. He was instrumental in getting the language of the people accepted as the Serbian literary language, and created a phonetic alphabet based on the principle: "Write as you speak, read as it is written".

In this agrarian land, which now began to revive and develop, class differentiation appeared, and with it the first bourgeois political parties. The existence of impoverished sections of the rural and urban population gave rise to the adoption of socialist ideas. The number of young intellectuals of liberal persuasion, educated abroad, steadily increased. Svetozar Marković (1846—1875) was the most forceful advocate of the new political and intellectual trend.

Around the turn of the century, industrial and economic development, although modest, led to the appearance of a proletariat. The Serbian Social Democratic Party was formed. Among the most prominent leaders of the workers' movement was Dimitrije Tucović, whose erudition, criticism of social relations and the expansionist plans of the Serbian

View of Belgrade from the Danube shore, lithography by K. Goebel, mid-19th century.

bourgeoisie, and principled attitude to the national question made him a noted figure in the international workers' movement.

The second decade of the 20th century brought the Balkan Wars. The Balkan states united to drive Turkey out of Macedonia, whose territory was divided among Serbia, Bulgaria and Greece. Dissatisfied with its share, Bulgaria attacked Serbia in 1913, but suffered defeat. Without a breathing-space, Serbia was attacked by the Austro-Hungarian armies in 1914, and so entered the First World War. Despite brilliant victories in the battles of Cer and Kolubara, the Serbian army was forced to withdraw south. After crossing Albania in conditions of untold hardship, the Serbian forces, halved in number, reached Greece in 1916. In the general offensive on the Salonica front in 1918, the Serbian army, together with the Allies, inflicted a decisive defeat on Austro-Hungarian, German and Bulgarian forces. After unparalleled suffering (the loss of one third of its population), Serbia emerged from the war victorious, and became part of the Kingdom of Serbs, Croats and Slovenes (later renamed the Kingdom of Yugoslavia) in 1918.

In this backward agricultural country, in which industry was mainly under the influence of foreign capital, the Court, aligned with the leading bourgeois circles, created a centralised and unitarist state, openly denying the national rights of the other South Slav nations and the national minorities.

Following the nazi occupation in April 1941, in July of the same year a nationwide uprising resulted in the liberation of an extensive area centred on the town of Užice (the "Užice Republic"), which was for a time the headquarters of the Supreme Command of the People's Liberation Army of Yugoslavia and its leader, Josip Broz Tito.

The development of Serbia after the Second World War aimed at transforming the country and the way of life of its citizens. Serbia now has over 1,500 work organisations (enterprises) with 38% of all employed persons in Yugoslavia. Parallel with the growth of industry, its agriculture has been modernised. New branches of industry have been established: electronics, automotive, cable, machine-tool and others.

Serbia has five universities (Belgrade, Novi Sad, Niš, Priština, Kragujevac), which graduated a total of around

114. *The spa of Vrnjačka Banja, a town of attractive parks and promenades lying at the foot of wooded Mt. Goč, is the most popular health and holiday resort in Serbia. The Romans built baths on this spot, where there are several medicinal springs used for both drinking and bathing.*

115. *Niš, Roman Naissus, the birthplace of Constantine the Great, is now the main city of eastern Serbia. Remains of luxurious Roman villas have been excavated at the nearby site of Mediana. Close to the city lies the spa of Niška Banja, a noted health resort with radio-active thermal springs. In the picture: part of the city centre.*

116. *Užice, a town in western Serbia, played a notable role in the early days of the liberation war, in the autumn of 1941, when it was the centre of the only liberated territory in occupied Europe, known as the "Užice Republic". Today this town of 77,000 inhabitants bears the name Titovo Užice.*

117. *In Novi Pazar, until the war one of the most backward areas of Serbia, efforts have been made to ensure that new buildings harmonise with the oriental atmosphere of the town. In the picture: the Vrbak Hotel.*

118. *Kragujevac, the centre of the automobile industry in Serbia, is a flourishing town of 165,000 with its own university. In the Second World War thousands of its inhabitants were executed in reprisals by the occupation forces.*

119. *Kruševac was the capital of the Serbian state at the end of the 14th century. The remains of the medieval fortress contrast with the modern buildings that have risen in Kruševac since the war.*

120. *On the highest plateau of Belgrade's Kalemegdan Fortress stands "The Victor", a work by the celebrated sculptor Ivan Meštrović. Across the Sava river from Kalemegdan stretches the new quarter of the city, Novi Beograd. In the picture: the building of the Museum of Modern Art in the foreground.*

121. *View of Belgrade from the Sava quay, a favourite promenade of its citizens.*

122. *The May 25 Museum, part of the Josip Broz Tito Memorial Centre in Belgrade, was built in 1962 as an exhibition place for the many gifts received by President Tito. The museum is also used for specialised exhibitions from the Memorial Centre collections.*

123. *The National Museum and National Theatre (1869) both face onto Republic Square in the centre of Belgrade, where there is also a statue of Prince Mihailo Obrenović.*

124. *Belgrade has played host to many important gatherings, some attended by several thousand participants. To meet the needs of large congresses, the ultra-modern Sava Centre has been built in Novi Beograd. Its main hall, seating 4,000, is used for various performances as well as congresses.*

125. *View across the Sava bridge towards the older part of Belgrade. The street running up from the bridge leads to Terazije Square and Prince Mihailo's Street (Knez Mihailova), the business and shopping centre of the Yugoslav capital.*

126. *After the war the marshes that lay across the Sava river, opposite Belgrade, were filled in with sand, and a whole new town, Novi Beograd, with 250,000 inhabitants, has been built here over the past three decades.*

390,000 students between 1955 and 1982, and 25 scientific-research institutes.

Belgrade (Beograd) is the capital of Yugoslavia and Serbia. Strategically placed at the confluence of the rivers Danube and Sava, it has a long and eventful history. Since the Second World War it has grown to four times the size — from less than 300,000 to over 1.4 million inhabitants. The site was first settled in the neolithic period. In the 3rd century BC, a Celtic tribe, the Scordisci, founded their stronghold of Singidunum here, mentioned under the name of Beograd for the first time in the 9th century. Located on two great rivers, between the fertile Pannonian Plain to the north and the hills of Šumadija to the south, it long lay on the frontier and defence line of mighty empires, paying for its strategic position by being razed to the ground 38 times. The Turks called it the "House of Wars". Its most notable historical monument is the ancient Kalemegdan Fortress. The city is mostly modern in its architecture, though there are a number of buildings from the period of the formation of the Serbian state in the 19th century. New Belgrade (Novi Beograd), the new quarter of the city on the left bank of the Sava, is one of the most ambitious building projects undertaken in Yugoslavia since the war.

Belgrade is an important economic and communications centre (junction of railways and highways linking Europe

Smederevo, lithograph by Erminy, 19th century.

and Asia, a river port, international airport), and also a centre of scientific, cultural and educational activity. It is the seat of the Serbian Academy of Sciences and Arts, and has its University, University of the Arts, opera and ballet companies, a number of theatres, and many scientific institutes, museums and art galleries. It hosts annual international festivals of the theatre (BITEF), film (FEST) and music (BEMUS). It has a large number of sports facilities: stadiums, halls, swimming pools, rowing courses, etc. and has been the venue of many major international sports competitions. Its position on two rivers, cultural monuments, and numerous cultural and sports events make it attractive to tourists.

Besides *Novi Sad* and *Priština*, the capitals of the two autonomous provinces, other major towns in Serbia are *Niš*, a university city, noted for its electronics, tobacco and engineering industries; *Kragujevac*, also with a university, the centre of the automobile industry; *Kraljevo, Titovo Užice, Valjevo, Šabac*, and *Zaječar*.

Serbia has many beautiful regions, some of them ideal for recreation, with a large number of mineral springs and spas — Vrnjačka, Niška, Mataruška, Bukovička, Koviljača and Sokobanja, which attract foreign as well as Yugoslav visitors. Winter and summer holidays can be spent on many of the mountains. The best known mountain resorts are on Kopaonik, Tara and Zlatibor.

Interesting excursions can be made to archaeological sites (Vinča, Viminacium, Gamzigrad — Romuliana, Caričin grad — Iustiniana Prima, Sirmium, Mediana, Ulpiana, Lepenski Vir and others). Renowned for their beauty are the river gorges (Djerdap — the largest gorge in Europe, Sićevačka, Vratna) and the caves (Resavska, Zlotska, Prekonoška). The many medieval monasteries and also monuments of Islamic architecture are of outstanding interest.

Vojvodina

Vojvodina, a socialist autonomous province within the Republic of Serbia, covers an area of 21,506 km² in the Pannonian Plain comprising the traditional districts of Banat, Bačka and almost all Srem. This fertile lowland is Yugoslavia's granary and has significant oil and natural gas resources.

At the time of the 1981 census, Vojvodina had 2,034,772 inhabitants: 1,107,375 Serbs (54.5 %), 385,356 ethnic Hungarians (19 %), 109,203 Croats (5.4 %), 69,549 Slovaks (3.4 %), 47,289 Romanians (2.3 %), 43,304 Montenegrins (2.1 %), 19,305 Ruthenians (0.9 %), 167,215 persons who declared themselves Yugoslavs (8.2 %), and 86,176 persons of other nationalities (4.3 %). Strict respect is paid to the legally-guaranteed equality of languages and scripts of the South Slav nations and other nationalities living on this territory: Serbo-Croatian (in the Serbian and Croatian variants), Hungarian, Slovakian, Romanian and Ruthenian.

This region inhabited by more than twenty different nationalities is a Europe in miniature. Radio Novi Sad broadcasts daily in five languages. Since the population includes settlers from all parts of the country, it is not unusual even for members of the same nationality to speak different dialects and have different traditional costumes and customs.

The geographical position of this region, the fertility of its soil and abundance of water served as a magnet from earliest times. Neolithic earth dwellings have yielded tools of polished stone, remains of grain and the bones of domestic animals, and also attractive figurines, altars and decorated pottery (the Starčevo site near Pančevo). From the copper age there are remains of graves and dwellings above ground (Gomolava), and from the bronze — jewelry of bronze and gold, daggers and battle-axes (Mokrin, Vatin).

The Romans ruled this territory for the first five centuries AD. In the city of Sirmium, whose remains have been excavated in the town of Sremska Mitrovica, they raised splendid buildings with mosaics, theatres, temples and baths. The city was laid waste and burnt by the Huns in the 5th century. After the disintegration of the Hunnish tribal alliance, the Gepids arrived here, to be followed in the 6th century by the Langobards, who withdrew into Italy before the advance of the Avars.

It was in this period that the Slavs entered the Panno-

127. *The fertile Vojvodina lowlands, part of the Pannonian Plain, are the country's biggest supplier of grain and industrial crops. Though arable farming takes first place, most farmers also raise some livestock. In the picture: a shepherd with his flock, a common sight on the outskirts of villages in Vojvodina.*

128. *Vojvodina is intersected by many waterways. The two great rivers of the plain, the Danube and Tisa, receive the waters of the Begej, Tamiš, Karaš and Nera, and of many canals. In the picture: part of the Danube—Tisa—Danube canal system, totalling 640 km of waterways.*

129. *Large fisheries have been constructed beside the Danube—Tisa—Danube canal system, whose waterways abound in a variety of fish, augmented by new species (amur, tolstolbik...) suited to these conditions.*

130. *Apart from sunflowers, the rich soil of Vojvodina yields large quantities of wheat, maize, sugar beet, hemp, hops, peppers, tobacco, and some flax and castor oil.*

131. *Still a feature of the broad Vojvodina landscape is the isolated farm (salaš), a cluster of buildings surrounded by an extensive area of arable land. Formerly the property of big landowners or well-to-do persons not engaged in farming, after the 1945 agrarian reform they were taken over by landless peasants, previously hired hands. In the picture: part of a salaš building with maize cobs.*

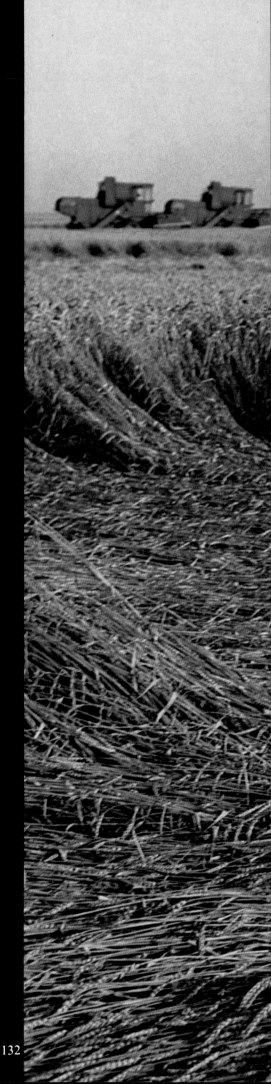

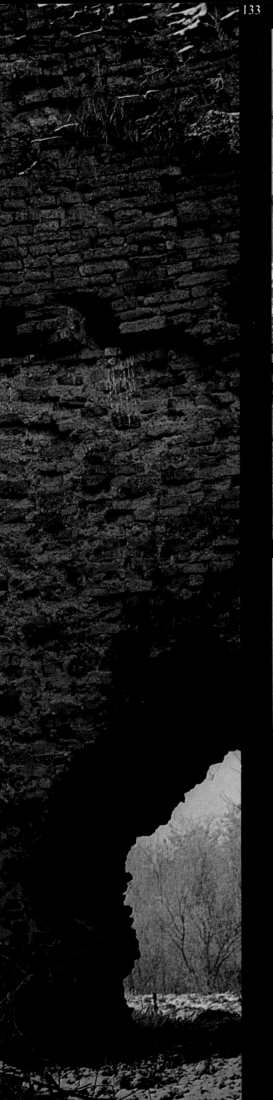

132. *Vojvodina, the most important agricultural region of Yugoslavia, supplies over one third of the total Yugoslav output of wheat, about two-thirds of its sugar beet, and over three-quarters of its sunflower crop. There are 1,627,000 hectares of arable land (1 hectare — c. 2.5 acres), of which 976,000 belong to private smallholdings. Farming is mechanised on the large agro-industrial estates (651,000 hectares), and on most of the smallholdings.*

133. *Bač Castle, formerly moated, from the early 14th century, stands near the village of Bač, on the Bačka Palanka—Sombor railway line. Now in a ruined state, it has five towers built of brick. The water for the moat was supplied by the river Mostong, which flows past it.*

134. *Petrovaradin Fortress, covering about 112 hectares on heights above the river Danube, was constructed in the 17th and 18th century according to the system of the famous French military engineer, Vauban. Across the river lies the city of Novi Sad.*

135. *Zrenjanin, a peaceful town on the river Begej, has many buildings whose architecture and imposing size capture the attention of visitors. Well preserved or successfully adapted to modern uses, they are the pride of its citizens.*

136. *Lake Palić near Subotica (4.2 km) underwent a unique ecological "operation" to save its life. Several years ago, after it was completely drained, its bed was cleaned and refilled with fresh water.*

nian Plain from the north-east. Following the collapse of Frankish rule, in the 10th century the nomadic Magyar people settled in the region. Their king, Istvan I, with the aid of German knights and western Christendom, laid the foundations of the feudal system here.

From the end of the 14th century, the penetration of the Turks into the Balkans resulted in the northward movement of Serbs. The Magyar (Hungarian) feudal lords accepted the refugees and used them as serfs and soldiers for the defence of the southern frontier, along the Sava and Danube. But the Turks conquered these regions too, holding them under their repressive rule from the first half of the 16th to the beginning of the 18th century (Banat until 1718).

Fleeing from Turkish reprisals, thousands of Serbs moved to Vojvodina in the great migration of 1690, led by Patriarch Arsenije III Čarnojević.

The Turkish defeat at Senta in 1697 by the forces of the Holy League (Austria, Poland, Venice) terminated a war that had lasted sixteen years. The peace treaty concluded in 1699 at Sremski Karlovci, known as the Peace of Karlovci (Karlowitz), marked the end of Turkish expansion towards the West and the onset of the decline in its military and political might.

Beočin Monastery, lithograph by an unknown artist, 19th century.

Over a lengthy period Austria undertook the resettlement (colonisation) of this fertile region laid waste by war. Besides Serbs, two Croatian ethnic groups — the Bunjevci and Šokci — were settled here. Special encouragement was given to the settlement of Germans, skilled craftsmen and farmers who used more advanced methods of tilling the land. Large numbers of Hungarians, Slovaks, Ruthenians and Romanians also came to live here.

Kuveždin Monastery, copperplate engraving by Z. Orfelin, 1772.

The Serbs in Vojvodina had more favourable conditions for developing cash-commodity relations than in Serbia. Parallel with the growth of capitalism and formation of a bourgeois class, there was a growing sense of national awareness and identity. The autonomy of Vojvodina was proclaimed in Sremski Karlovci in 1848, but abolished in 1860, when the region was handed over to Hungary. Bourgeois liberals, under the leadership of Svetozar Miletić (1826—1901) continued the struggle for autonomy, constitutional liberty, political rights and national equality. In the 1870s the socialist movement began to gain support. After the First World War, Vojvodina became part of the Kingdom of Serbs, Croats and Slovenes, later renamed Yugoslavia.

After the capitulation of the Kingdom of Yugoslavia in 1941, Vojvodina was split into three: Bačka was annexed by fascist Hungary, Srem was incorporated in the quisling puppet state known as the Independent State of Croatia, while Banat, formally under the quisling regime in Serbia, was in fact controlled by the local German population. However, the nations and nationalities of this province never reconciled themselves to alien and fascist rule. Under the leadership of the Communist Party of Yugoslavia, they began to organise Partisan units, and fought in all parts of Yugoslavia.

Novi Sad (pop. c. 258,000), the capital of Vojvodina, lies on the river Danube. It developed from the small settlement of Petrovaradinski Šanac, raised in 1694 across the river from the huge Petrovaradin Fortress. On February 1, 1748, it was proclaimed a royal free city and took its present name (Latin: Neoplanta). Novi Sad's well-preserved old quarter recalls the age of craft guilds, merchants and bargemasters, the time when Serbian poets, painters, journalists and politicians, together with socialist rebels who had fled from Serbia and Bulgaria, engaged in passionate debates, made ardent

137. *An old windmill near Čurug, a place on the river Tisa in the Bačka district. Now a rarity and protected by law, mills like these were once a feature of the broad, windy Pannonian lowlands.*

138. *Vrdnik, one of numerous Serbian Orthodox monasteries raised in the Fruška Gora hills (539 m) in the district of Srem, south of the Danube. It takes its name from the nearby village of Vrdnik, but is also called Ravanica, since it was restored in the 17th century by monks from the monastery of Ravanica in Serbia. Vrdnik has a rich treasury and keeps the casket of Prince Lazar, who was killed leading the Serbs in the battle of Kosovo in 1389.*

139. *Beočin monastery in Srem, restored in the early 18th century by monks from the monastery of Rača on the Drina, who were renowned as manuscript copyists.*

140. *The cathedral church in Vršac, a town 12 km from the Romanian frontier, has a fine iconostasis from 1805—1807 by the well-known painter Pavel Djurković.*

141. *Most places in Vojvodina still have open-air markets where local farmers sell their produce. In the picture: the market close to the baroque church of St George in Sombor.*

142. *Wall painting in the church of Bodjani monastery, the work of Hristofor Žefarović (1737). This Serbian Orthodox monastery, south of Sombor, was founded in the 15th century, but most of its present buildings, including the church, are from the 18th.*

143. *Zrenjanin, formerly called Veliki Bečkerek and then Petrovgrad, is first mentioned in the 14th century. The largest town in the Banat district, it has flourishing food-processing industries. Notable buildings include the baroque Orthodox church (1779) and Town Hall (in the picture).*

Hopovo Monastery, lithograph by an unknown 19th-century artist.

speeches, wrote patriotic poems and articles, and dreamt of national liberty. During the 19th century, the city was the most important centre of Serbian culture, "the Serbian Athens" as it was called in Europe. It has the oldest Serbian theatre (1861), and an eminent cultural and scholarly society known as Matica srpska (founded in 1826). The high schools of Karlovci (1791) and Novi Sad (1810) and many other schools, including the Sombor Teachers' College (1778), paved the way for the foundation of Novi Sad University (1960).

Subotica, second in size, is a typical Pannonian town with an economy based on its agricultural surroundings but also on well-developed industry. *Zrenjanin* is a centre of the food-processing industry, while *Pančevo* is best known for its chemical industry. *Sombor* is noted for its arts and music festivals, and for the gallery displaying the works of the contemporary painter Milan Konjović, *Kikinda* for its nearby deposits of oil, natural gas and clay, *Vršac* for the extensive vineyards on its nearby hill and its wine festival, and *Sremska Mitrovica* as the site of Sirmium, founded in the 1st century, which was one of the major cities of the Roman Empire from the 3rd century.

Villages in Vojvodina are of the Pannonian type, with long broad streets flanked mostly by one-story dwellings.

Many have a multi-national character. The movements into this fertile region, which still continue, and especially the large-scale colonisation in the 18th and 19th centuries and after both world wars, have created an ethnically mixed population. In the large village of Crvenka, for instance, no less than 24 nationalities live together.

Vojvodina is the most important agricultural region in Yugoslavia, providing over half the marketed supplies of food — one third of the wheat, 65 % of sugar beet, 55 % of pork, 30 % of beef, and large amounts of other produce.

Of the 1,627,000 hectares of arable land (1 hectare = c. 2.5 acres), 40 % is socially owned, while the remainder is in the hands of smallholders, many of whom cooperate with the large socially-owned farms. The extensive Danube—Tisa—Danube system of waterways, built between 1957 and 1977, besides draining off surplus water, allows the irrigation of up to 400,000 hectares of fertile land, making it possible to raise two harvests annually and ensuring high and stable production. Thanks to scientific advances, particularly in the creation of new high-yielding varieties, Vojvodina is noted for its large output of wheat, maize and industrial crops (sugar beet, sunflower). The annual International Agricultural Fair in

144. *Subotica (pop. 155,000), close to the Hungarian frontier, was founded in the early 16th century. The old part of the town is a pleasing architectural entity with the Town Hall from the turn of the century, the baroque Catholic church of St Theresa and an Orthodox church from the early 18th century.*
In the picture: part of the Town Hall in Subotica.

145. *Panorama of Sremski Karlovci, a small baroque town on the right bank of the Danube, close to the Fruška Gora hills. In the 18th and 19th centuries it was an important cultural and educational centre of the Serbs in Vojvodina, and was long the seat of the Patriarch of the Serbian Orthodox Church. Its notable buildings include the patriarch's palace and chapel with an iconostasis painted by Uroš Predić (1857—1953), the cathedral church, the so-called Upper and Lower churches, the Peace chapel and the building of the oldest Serbian high school, opened in 1791.*

146. *A street in the village of Uzdin, in Banat, with the varied façades typical of Vojvodina villages. Together with the village of Kovačica, Uzdin is noted as a centre of naive painting in Vojvodina. The peasant-women painters of Uzdin have often exhibited abroad.*

147. *The building of the Banat Eparchy in Vršac, a town lying at the foot of Vršac Hill (641 m). Built in the 18th century, it is generally known as the Bishop's Palace.*

148. *Besides its old quarter, Novi Sad has several new suburbs and a number of modern university buildings and broad boulevards. In the picture: the building of the Federal Executive Council (Government) of Vojvodina in Novi Sad.*

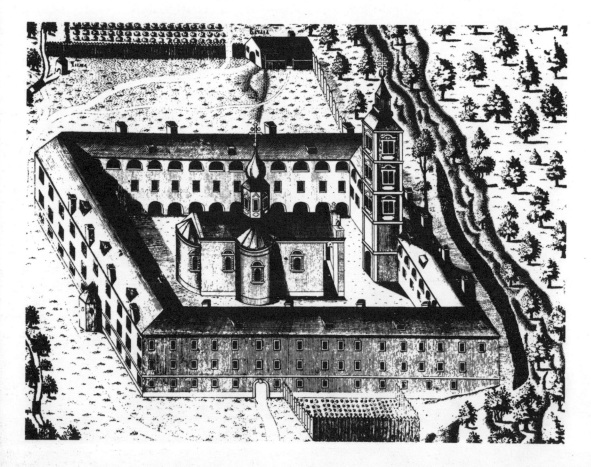

Krušedol Monastery, copperplate engraving by Z. Orfelin, 1775.

139

140

141

142

149. *Novi Sad, capital of Vojvodina, stretching along the bank of the Danube, was founded at the end of the 17th century as a bridgehead to guard the pontoon bridge connecting Petrovaradin Fortress with the left bank of the river. When it was proclaimed a royal free town in 1748, it was named Neoplanta, which the Serbs translated as Novi Sad. In the picture: Novi Sad cathedral.*

150. *In the centre of Novi Sad stands the monument to Svetozar Miletić (1826—1901), leader of the Serbs in their struggle for national emancipation in the Austro-Hungarian state.*

151. *The old centre of Novi Sad has retained its 19th-century atmosphere.*

152. *Several charming architectural ensembles have been preserved in Novi Sad. Notable buildings include the 19th-century neo-Gothic cathedral with a carved wooden iconostasis with paintings by Paja Jovanović (1859—1957), the former Town Hall and many pleasing residential buildings.*

153, 154. *A feature of Vojvodina is its ethnic diversity. Its inhabitants belong to over twenty different nationalities — hence the variety of traditional costumes.*
In the pictures: scene in a courtyard, and houses in the Slovakian village of Kovačica.

155. *The surroundings of Vršac are a noted wine-growing area. Every autumn, vintage festivities are celebrated in the town.*
In the picture: scene of the vintage celebrations in Vršac in front of the neo-Gothic Town Hall.

156. *The spacious houses of Vojvodina's farmers have barns, stables and pig-sties alongside, for smallholders engage in livestock as well as arable farming.*

The Battle of Slankamen, 1691, lithograph (detail).

Novi Sad provides a showcase for achievements in this branch of the economy.

Arable and livestock farming form the basis for the development of the food-processing industry — sugar refineries, breweries, industrial slaughter-houses, mills, and factories producing edible oil, tinned food, biscuits, prepared meals, medicaments, textiles footwear and other goods based on agricultural raw materials.

Vojvodina is also a wine- and fruit-growing region, exporting mainly apples and peaches. The wines of the Fruška Gora and Vršac areas enjoy a high reputation.

Besides its highly-developed agriculture, in the postwar period, Vojvodina has built up considerable industry, which now accounts for 41.8 % of the province's gross material product. This includes petroleum, natural gas and petrochemical production, metalworking, engineering and electronics, building materials, food-processing, textiles, woodworking and shipbuilding.

Some 70 % of Yugoslavia's navigable waterways are in Vojvodina — 732 km of rivers and 646 km of canals. Easily accessible from all directions, Vojvodina serves as a natural bridge between Europe and the Middle East.

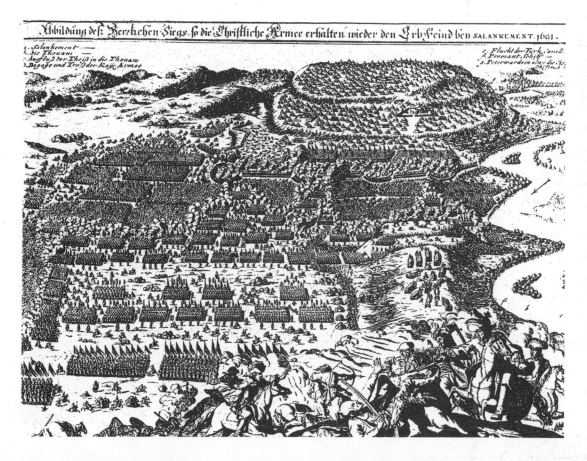

176

All children of school age attend primary school, and
receive instruction in their mother tongue, at the same time
learning one of the other languages spoken in their environ-
ment. Vojvodina at present has 15 university faculties, one
art academy and 13 two-year colleges, attended by over
35,000 students all told. The faculties have their own scientific institutes which work on projects aimed at promoting
production and advances in industry. All the various nationalities have highly developed cultural activities. About one
thousand titles are published annually in the languages used
in Vojvodina, in a total of some four million copies. Vojvodina
has its own Academy of Sciences and Arts.

The natural wealth and specific configuration of Vojvodina — its great rivers, canals, excellent hunting and fishing,
spas — offer favourable conditions for tourism. There are
many places of cultural and historical interest (Petrovaradin
Fortress, Bač Fortress, the monasteries of the Fruška Gora
area) and cultural institutions (the Matica srpska Gallery,
collections of Yugoslav and foreign artists and the Museum
of the Revolution in Novi Sad, and other galleries and
museums elsewhere). The Obedska bara and Carska bara
marshes and Ludoško lake are well-known reserves of marsh
birds.

The Fruška Gora National Park, a hilly area stretching
along the Danube, with rare examples of flora and fauna and
a large number of monasteries, is a highly popular excursion
and recreation centre. The Deliblatska peščara (sands),
formerly a region of shifting sands known as the "European
Sahara", covers an area of 300 km^2 in the south of the Banat
district. The arms of the Danube and its sandy islands are
delightful for boating and camping trips. Lake Palić (4.2 km^2),
close to Subotica, whose water was drained in order to clean
the lake bed (a unique ecological undertaking), is among the
most attractive and well-arranged resorts of Central European type.

Kosovo

Kosovo is a socialist autonomous province within the Republic of Serbia, covering an area of 10,908 km^2. At the time of the 1981 census it had 1,584,440 inhabitants: 1,226,736 ethnic Albanians (77.3 %), 209,497 Serbs (13.3 %), 58,562 Moslems (3.7 %), 27,028 Montenegrins (1.7 %), 14,539 Romanies (0.9 %), 12,513 ethnic Turks (0.8 %), 2,676 persons who declared themselves Yugoslavs (0.2 %) and 32,889 persons of other nationalties (2.1 %). In government administration, education and public life the Serbo-Croatian and Albanian languages are used, and in areas with an ethnic Turkish population, the Turkish language also.

The birthrate, which was 25.2 per thousand in the 1981—1985 period, and density of population — 145.6 inhabitants per square kilometre (1981), are the highest in Yugoslavia.

The region comprises two extensive depressions: the Kosovo Plain, mainly around the rivers Ibar and Sitnica; and the Metohija Plain, drained by the river Beli Drim, both encircled by mountains: the Kopaonik massif (highest peak: Oštro koplje, 1,789 m) in the north, Mt. Šara (Šarplanina, with peaks of 2,496, 2,587 and 2,640 m), the slopes of the Skopska Crna Gora and other mountains in the south, Prokletije (with the Djeravica peak, 2,656 m) in the west, and lower mountains around the upper Morava valley (Pomoravlje) in the east. The former volcanic area — the Trepča district with the

157. *The slopes of Mt. Šara are increasingly popular with winter sports enthusiasts. The construction of roads, hotels and ski-lifts have created conditions for the fuller exploitation of its fine skiing terrains.*
In the picture: an area of Mt. Šara not far from the winter sports resort of Brezovica.

158. *The road from Peć leading to Montenegro (across the Čakor pass, 1,849 m) runs through the magnificent Rugovo gorge, 10 km in length, carved out by the swift-flowing Pećka Bistrica, abundant in trout. Every turn in this road, which follows the winding river between cliffs several hundred metres high in places, reveals yet another breath-taking vista. The Rugovo area is noted for its striking traditional men's costume (made of white homespun with black braiding, and worn with a white cloth turban) and for its exciting folk dances.*

159. *The mausoleum (turbeh) of Sultan Murat, not far from Priština, was raised, according to tradition, on the spot where he was killed during the battle of Kosovo in 1389.*

160. *The monastery church of the Holy Archangels, one the largest and most splendid buildings of its time, was raised by Emperor Dušan of Serbia between 1348 and 1352 in the gorge of the Prizrenska Bistrica river.*

Priština, etching by T. Krizman, 1915.

164

165

161. *Sinan-pasha's mosque in Prizren, early 17th century, in the classical Ottoman style, was built of white marble blocks brought from the ruined 14th-century church of the Holy Archangels. One of the most impressive mosques from this period, it is notable for its rich oriental-style ornamentation.*

162. *The monastery of the Patriarchate of Peć, near the town of Peć, has three churches dedicated to the Holy Apostles (13th c., which became the seat of the Serbian archbishopric in 1253), St Demetrius (14th c.) and the Virgin Hodeghetria (14th. c.). The earliest frescoes are in the oldest church and date from the 13th century, when fresco-painting reached its full maturity. The names of the artists are unknown.*

163. *The wall painting in the church of Gračanica monastery belongs to a style influenced by manuscript illumination, though traces of the earlier monumental style can be seen in the elegant movements and suppleness of the figures. In the picture: a 14th-century fresco in the narthex of the monastery church with a portrait of Queen Simonida.*

164. *The majority of the inhabitants of Kosovo today are ethnic Albanians. In the Middle Ages Serbian rulers founded many churches of outstanding architectural value in this region (the Patriarchate of Peć, Dečani, Gračanica, St Mary Ljeviška). A mosque and an Orthodox church standing side by side in Uroševac symbolise this shared heritage.*

extinct volcano Zvečan, the Novo Brdo-Janjevo district and others — is one of the main mining regions of Yugoslavia. Half of Kosovo's one million hectares is wooded, 185,000 hectares are pasture, and about 400,000 hectares arable land.

The provincial capital is Priština, with c. 210,000 inhabitants. Other sizable towns include Prizren, Peć, Titova Mitrovica, Djakovica, Gnjilane and Uroševac.

Archaeological excavations have revealed that the Kosovo region was populated in the stone age, and that its earliest known inhabitants were the Illyrians. Ancient Illyrian remains include the stronghold of Ulpiana near Priština, tumuli at Romaja near Prizren, and the ruins of a stronghold on the outskirts of present-day Peć.

In ancient times, Kosovo, like the rest of the Balkans, attracted numerous conquerors, above all the Romans and Byzantines. In the 6th and 7th centuries, the Slavs settled in the Balkans. Until the 11th century, Kosovo was a border region of the Byzantine Empire. In the late 12th century, the Serbian ruler, Stefan Nemanja, extended his realm to include the whole of Kosovo. Until it fell under Turkish rule, Kosovo was the central region of the Serbian medieval state. For a time, Prizren was the capital of the Serbian Empire of Dušan and Uroš, while Peć was the seat of the Serbian Patriarchate (proclaimed in 1346). After the famous battle of Koso-

The Battle of Kosovo, lithograph by A. Stefanović, 1875.

vo fought on this territory in 1389, control passed to the Turks.

Many buildings and remains from this period have come down to us, including the ruins of Novo Brdo (estimated to have had 35,000 inhabitants), the most important settlement and stronghold. There are also many churches and monasteries: the church of St Mary Ljeviška in Prizren (built in 1307 on the foundations of a Byzantine church); the church of the Holy Archangels (14th c.), surrounded by defensive walls, near Prizren; the monastery church of Visoki Dečani (14th c.), the largest and most splendid Romanesque building in medieval Serbia, with outstanding frescoes; Gračanica monastery (c. 1310) near Priština, an original variant of the Serbo-Byzantine architectural style; Banjska monastery (14th c.) near Titova Mitrovica, and others. Of particular interest is the complex of the Patriarchate of Peć, at the entrance to the Rugovo Gorge, with the churches of the Holy apostles (1253), St Demetrius (1324) and the Virgin Mary (14th c.), and other buildings.

From the Turkish period, a considerable number of fine mosques remain: the Fatih mosque (1461) in Priština, Sinanpasha's mosque (17th c.) in Prizren, the Hadum mosque (16th

165. *The architecture and painting of the monasteries and churches of the golden age of medieval Serbian art are complemented by the beautiful stone-carving adorning portals and windows.*

166. *Gračanica monastery on the Kosovo plain, not far from Priština, is the most outstanding example of the Serbo-Byzantine style of architecture in the country. A foundation of King Milutin of Serbia (1320), with its façade of red and yellow ashlar and domes rising steplike, one above the other, it leaves a truly harmonious and monumental impression.*

167. *Seated anthropomorphic figurine of baked red clay, from the late neolithic period (second half of the 3rd millennium BC), found in Priština and now kept in the Kosovo Museum, Priština.*

Prizren, etching by D. Kokotović, 1914.

c.) in Djakovica, the Bajrakli mosque (16th c.) in Peć and others. There are also numerous baths, tekkes (monasteries) and turbehs (tombs), such as Sultan Murat's and the Gazi-Mestan turbeh both near Priština.

After their victory in the battle of Kosovo (1389), the Turks began to convert the population to Islam. The oppressive economic, social and political conditions under Turkish rule led the people to rebel many times in the 16th, 17th and 18th centuries, particularly during the wars between the western powers and Turkey. This resulted in closer ties and cooperation between the Balkan nations, especially the Albanians and Serbs.

Strong national liberation movements appeared in the Balkans in the 19th century, giving rise to the first and second Serbian uprisings against the Turks and the formation among the Albanians of the Prizren League (1878), which led the Albanian movement for liberation from Ottoman subjection. Kosovo was freed from Turkish rule in 1912, at the end of the First Balkan War, when it was returned to Serbia.

At the end of the First World War, Kosovo became part of the Kingdom of Serbs, Croats and Slovenes, later renamed Yugoslavia, in which it was the most backward region, in consequence of its inherited socio-economic conditions. This was apparent in all aspects of life — its extensive farming methods, lack of industry, unexploited energy resources, primitive level of crafts and communications, few schools and small number of Albanian children able to obtain any education, the high rate of illiteracy among the population, and the generally low cultural level.

Social problems remained unresolved, and the agrarian question, which was the most acute since poor peasants made up the bulk of the population, was dealt with in a particularly unsatisfactory manner. The position of the Albanian section of the population was especially hard.

During the Second World War, the territory of Kosovo was occupied by German, Bulgarian and Italian forces. Answering the call to arms of the Communist Party of Yugoslavia in 1941, Partisan units were formed, composed of Albanians, Serbs, Montenegrins, Macedonians and others.

In view of the multi-national structure of the population and the region's specific historical and cultural background, and in accordance with the freely expressed will of the people, the Autonomous Kosovo-Metohija Region was established as part of the Republic of Serbia in 1945, becoming the Socialist Autonomous Province of Kosovo within Serbia in 1968.

In the postwar period, Kosovo has recorded notable results in its socio-economic development and has steadily modernised its economy. It is no longer simply a producer of raw materials and power; processing and manufacturing industries are rapidly expanding as well. The main branches are the rubber, food-processing, textile, metalworking and electrical goods industries, and the production of artificial fertilizers.

Kosovo has lignite reserves estimated at around 10,000 million tons. The large thermal power plants built in this region have a capacity of 1,400 MW.

The economic progress of Kosovo is closely bound up with the development of the Trepča Mining, Metallurgical and Chemical Works, Kosovo's industrial giant, and one of Europe's leading lead and zinc producers.

The climate and soil are favourable for agriculture. In addition to smaller projects, two large multi-purpose water

168. *Through the centuries, the industrious fingers of weavers and tailors have embellished the traditional costumes to suit the tastes and needs of the various ethnic and religious groups of the region. The rich variety of such costumes can best be seen in towns on market days.*

169. *The old part of Prizren has retained much of its 19th-century atmosphere with its uneven cobblestones, small houses topped by chimneys, and little cafés where the smoke of charcoal grills heralds an evening of sociable talk and song.*

170. *The number of different ethnic groups accounts for the wide variety of traditional costumes in Kosovo. There are more than thirty in this province, many of which have retained their authentic features and are still worn, especially in rural areas.*

171. *The building in Prizren that was once the headquarters of the Prizren League is now a museum housing exhibits and documents from the time of its foundation (1878).*

172. *The colourful folk costumes, differing greatly from one ethnic group to the next, add to the charm of the traditional dances, likewise remarkable for their diversity. In the picture: the Prizren Wedding dance.*

173. *The small crafts shops in Priština with their skilfully-made articles still survive the flood of industrial goods. The craftsman, with the inevitable pipe, quietly awaits his customers, perhaps with a touch of nostalgia for busier times.*

Gračanica Monastery, woodcut, 1539.

174. *Below the ancient Kaljaja Fortress lies the well-preserved old urban centre of Prizren, mostly dating from the first half of the 19th century. The part of the town on the left bank of the river Bistrica and certain buildings in other parts have been placed under state protection.*

175. *Modern architecture predominates in the centre of almost all towns of any size in Kosovo. Its design, however, often incorporates features inspired by oriental influences, long present on this territory. In the picture: a department store in Peć.*

176. *A group of young people at an exhibition of modern tapestries in Priština.*

177. *Priština, the capital of Kosovo, is a modern city with many new buildings of architectural interest. One of these is the Culture Centre named after Bora Vukmirović and Ramiz Sadiq, a Serb and an Albanian who fell side by side in the National Liberation War.*

178. *The new building of the Library in Priština successfully combines contemporary architectural trends with elements of the traditional local building style.*

179. *Priština is a city of the young — more than half its inhabitants are under thirty. The university faculties and two-year colleges in the town have about 40,000 full-time students.*

180. *Albanian folk dances are mostly graceful and dignified. Many folklore groups keep alive the musical traditions of the Albanian people. In the picture: an Albanian folk dance from the Rugovo area.*

regulation systems have been constructed (the Ibar and Radonjić), which will make it possible to achieve higher yields and more modern organisation of agricultural production. Kosovo wine, produced on 5,000 hectares of large-scale vineyards and mostly exported, is well known for its quality.

In consequence of adverse historical, economic and social conditions in the past, Kosovo is the most underdeveloped part of Yugoslavia. Dynamic socio-economic progress has resulted in an appreciable rise in the *per capita* income. All the country's economic plans attach special importance to the accelerated development of Kosovo, which receives about half of the total resources of the federal fund for the faster growth of the underdeveloped regions.

It is in the fields of education and culture that the heavy legacy of the past has left its strongest imprint. On the eve of the war, 80 % of the population were illiterate. There was no form of education or cultural activity in the languages of the non-South Slav nationalities.

Today, every third person in the province is acquiring education. Primary and secondary schools are attended by 430,000 young Albanians, Serbs, Montenegrins, Turks and Moslems . . . University faculties and two-year colleges have

Prizren, pencil sketch by Lj. Ivanović, 1919.

a total enrolment of 40,000 full-time and part-time students.

Parallel with the spread of education, the foundations have been laid for more rapid cultural transformation and the fostering of culture in general, particularly in those domains neglected in the past.

Priština became a university city in 1960, and has a number of other important cultural and scientific institutions: the Academy of Sciences and Arts, University Library, Provincial Theatre, museums, art galleries and archives.

Newspapers and periodicals are published in three languages, in which Priština's radio and television stations also broadcast.

Kosovo is a region of great scenic beauty, with many well-stocked hunting grounds, mineral springs, beautiful caves and fine ski slopes. The cultural and historical monuments and remains from prehistoric times down to the present day are a further attraction for tourists. Its geographical position, network of modern roads and airport at Priština have contributed to the growth of transit tourism. Modern hotels have been constructed, and Brezovica on Mt. Šara has become a popular winter sport centre.

Montenegro (Crna Gora) covers an area of 13,712 km², and at the time of the 1981 census had 584,310 inhabitants; 400,488 Montenegrins (69 %), 78,000 Moslems (13.2 %), 37,736 ethnic Albanians (6.2 %), 19,407 Serbs (3.3 %), 6,904 Croats (1.2 %), 31,243 persons who declared themselves Yugoslavs (5.3 %), and 10,533 persons of other nationalities (1.8 %).

Most of Montenegro is mountainous, with severe snowy winters, while the southern regions along the Adriatic coast and around Lake Skadar enjoy a mild Mediterranean climate. The lowlands are along the river Zeta and the lower course of the Morača, and around Lake Skadar (391 km², of which 243 km² belong to Yugoslavia).

The south-west part consists of barren rocky uplands. In the north rise the high Dinaric Mts. — Durmitor (2,523 m), Ljubišnja (2,238 m), Volujak with Bioče (2,396 m), Sinjajevina (2,203 m), Bjelasica (2,139 m), Komovi (2,487 m) and Maganik (2,139 m). Along the coast rise Mts. Lovćen (1,749 m), Orjen (1,895 m) and Rumija (1,593 m).

Crkvice (1,100 m above sea level) on Orjen, above the Gulf of Kotor, is notable for having the highest rainfall in Europe: an annual average of 4,500—5,000 mm (in the record year of 1937—8,065 mm).

The coastal part of Montenegro stretches south from the Gulf of Kotor (Boka Kotorska), an exceptional beautiful series of submerged valleys, resembling a fjord, cutting into the Orjen and Lovćen massifs, down to the mouth of the river Bojana (the frontier with Albania). The coastline is fairly indented and has numerous good beaches.

The territory of present-day Montenegro was inhabited in prehistoric times, as testified by remains of material culture (notably those at Crvena Stijena, not far from Nikšić).

In the 3rd century BC Illyrian tribes had a powerful state here, conquered a century later by the Romans, who ruled the region for several centuries. Ruins of the Roman city of Doclea (Duklja) can be seen near Titograd.

After settling in these parts in the 7th century, the Slavs founded their state, at first called Duklja and then Zeta (after the river). Later Zeta was for a time part of Raška (Serbia) and Macedonia, and after the fall of the Macedonian emperor, Samuilo, came under Byzantine rule. This was a time of many fierce clashes with the Byzantine army (the most famous battles were at Crmnica and Bar in 1042). At the

181. *As its name suggests, Montenegro is a mountainous land. Of the many towering massifs that extend right down to the coast, Mt. Durmitor (2,522 m), covered with dense beech and pine forests, holds a special place in the heart of Montenegrins, symbolising their defiance of all invaders. In the picture: Mt. Durmitor.*

182. *The area of Lake Skadar, encircled by mountains, enjoys a mild Mediterranean climate, being separated from the sea only by Mts. Sutorman (1,182 m), Rumija (1,593 m) and Sozina (1,186 m). This is the largest lake in the Balkans (391 km²), two-thirds of it lying in Montenegro, and the rest in Albania.*

Many historical remains are scattered around its shores on its islands: Illyrian burial grounds, small medieval churches, monasteries, fortresses ... The lake has an abundance of fish (lake sardine, carp, eel, trout) and birds (wild duck, geese, pelicans).

In the picture: panorama of Lake Skadar.

183. *Below Obod hill, where the Crnojević printing press was located at the end of the 15th century, rises the Crnojević river (Rijeka Crnojevića), which flows into Lake Skadar only a few kilometres away. When water chestnuts cover its calm waters, the local flat-bottomed boats force channels through the aquatic plants, creating the illusion of rivers and canals on its green surface.*

184. *Just above the Gulf of Kotor and Lake Skadar, beginning from the massifs of Orjen (1,895 m) and Lovćen (1,749 m), stretches the barren rocky region known as the "sea of stone". In this endless arid wilderness, the only signs of human habitation are a few clusters of stone dwellings or isolated cottages surrounded by small patches of greenery. For centuries the tough Montenegrin peasants of this area defended their homes and freedom from Turkish incursions and raids.*

In the picture: view of the Katun area.

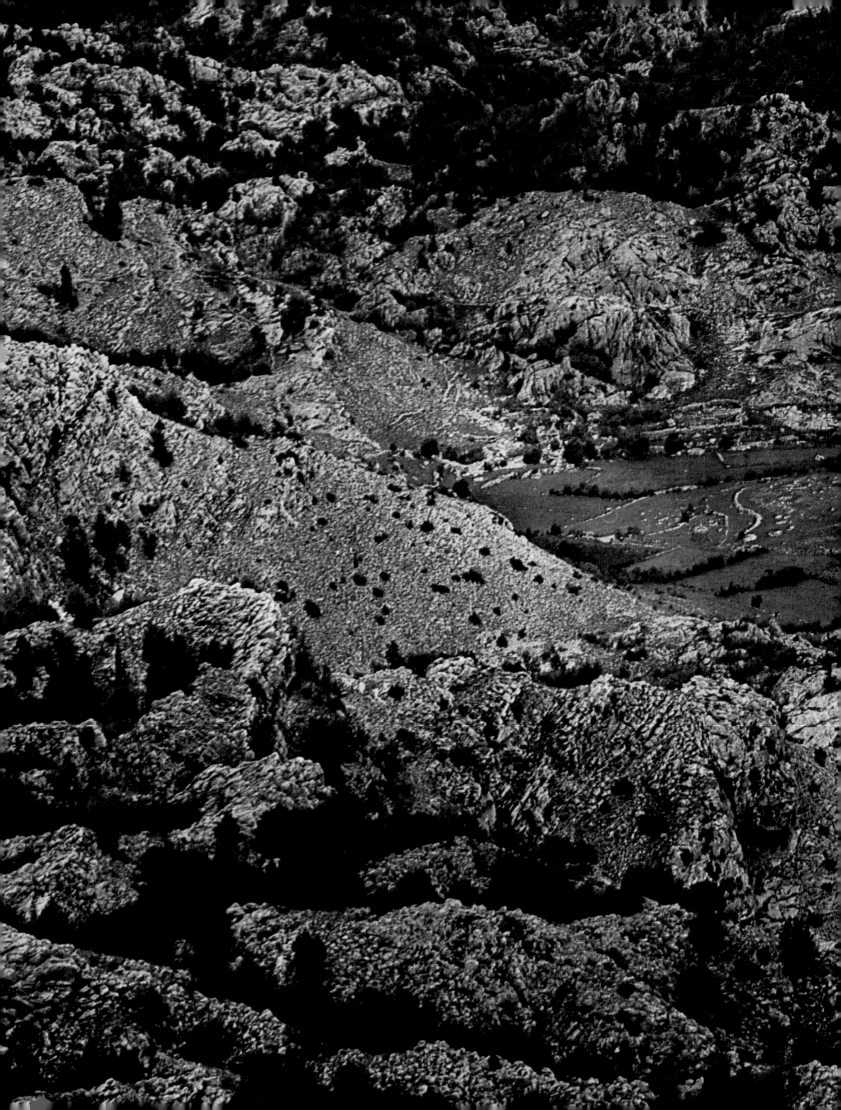

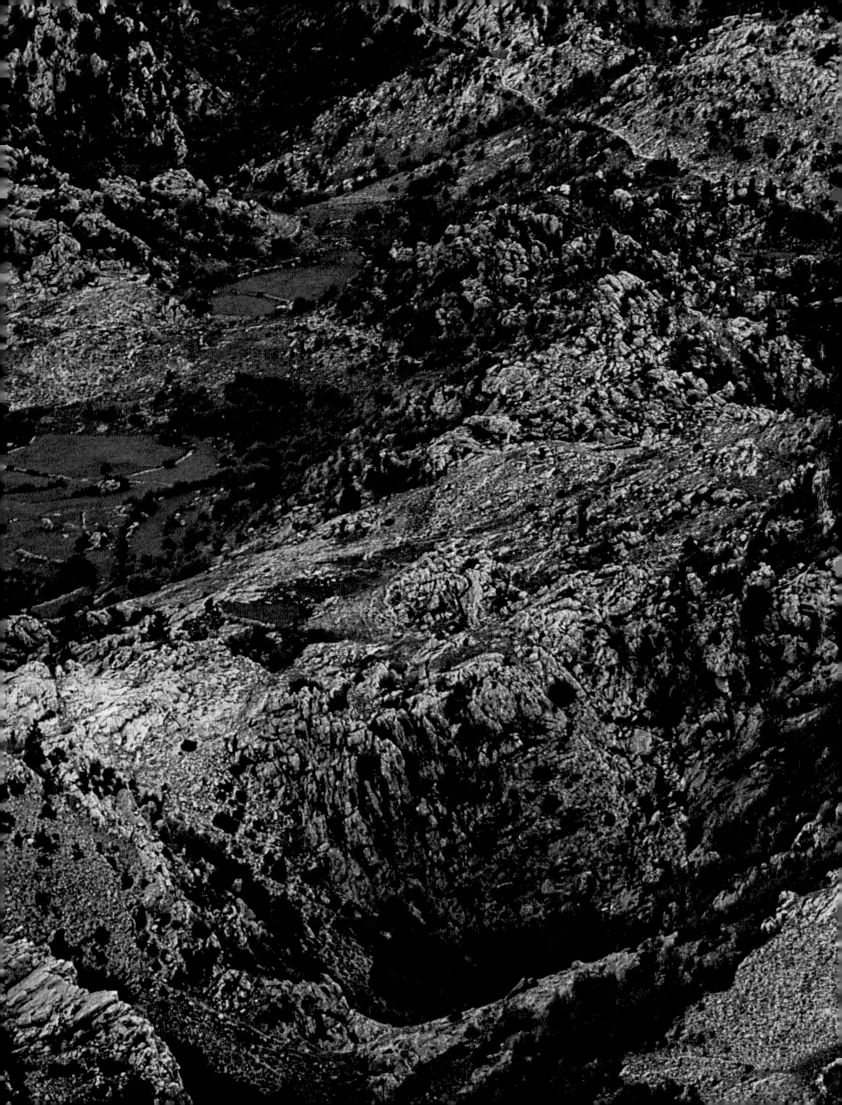

185. *The magnificent Gulf of Kotor (Boka kotorska) with the Orjen and Lovćen massifs rising steeply from its shores is unrivalled in the Adriatic for its scenic beauty. The old towns and villages around the Gulf — Herceg-Novi, Risan, Perast, Kotor and Tivat — have many fine old buildings and historical monuments, an additional attraction of this fascinating corner of the Adriatic. In the picture: panorama of the Gulf of Kotor.*

186. *Part of Kotor, an ancient town lying at the innermost point of the Gulf of Kotor. It is surrounded by massive walls, up to 10 metres high, which climb the steep slopes behind the town to the hill (260 m) with the fort of St John (Sveti Jovan). Once a Roman settlement of strategic significance (Akurion, Aeruvium, Catarum), it grew in the Middle Ages into a prosperous city with a powerful fleet, and was for a time a republic.*
The finest among its old buildings is the Romanesque aisled cathedral of St Tryphon (Sveti Tripun), built in 1166.

187. *Panorama of Cetinje, former capital of Montenegro, lying in a karst depression on the Lovćen massif. In the 15th century the Montenegrin ruler Ivan Crnojević moved his capital from Lake Skadar to this mountain fastness, less vulnerable to Turkish attacks. He built a residence for himself (1482) and a monastery dedicated to the Virgin Mary (1484), and moved his printing press here from Obod. From that time on, Cetinje became the stronghold of Montenegrin resistance to Turkish might. It was the seat of the Montenegrin bishop-princes, and later the capital of the principality, afterwards kingdom of Montenegro.*

end of the 12th century, the Serbian ruler, Stefan Nemanja, incorporated Zeta into his realm. Under the Serbian kings of the Nemanjić dynasty, right down to Emperor Dušan, Zeta enjoyed autonomy. After Dušan's death (1355), it was once more an independent state, ruled in turn by the Balšić and Crnojević families. Zeta managed to retain its independence in a "precarious equilibrium" between Turkey and Venice. This tiny state (known as Crna Gora from the middle of the 14th century) was constantly compelled to defend itself from the Turks, and had to move its capital from Žabljak on Lake Skadar to a less vulnerable site — Cetinje — in the mountains.

A centuries-long struggle for independence and against recognition of Turkish authority was waged by the Montenegrin tribes led and inspired by their bishop-princes (*vladike*), holders of both spiritual and temporal power in Montenegro down to the time of Prince Danilo (1851—1860), who renounced his religious authority. He was succeeded by Prince, later King Nikola Petrović (1860—1918), during whose reign Montenegro gained international recognition as a sovereign state.

The small, impoverished country, whose boundaries had been extended by the return of part of its occupied territory, now made some economic progress, with the building of

Cetinje Monastery, lithograph, late 19th—early 20th century.

roads, the first railway (from Bar to Virpazar) and a port at Bar, the opening of a number of small factories and workshops, and the introduction of a motorised postal service.

Its development was interrupted by the liberation wars in the second half of the 19th century. Montenegrins again took up arms in the First and Second Balkan Wars (1912 and 1913), and then in the First World War (1914—1918). Despite major Montenegrin successes, particularly the victory in the battle of Mojkovac which facilitated the withdrawal of the Serbian army, Austro-Hungarian forces occupied Montenegro in 1916.

From 1918 Montenegro formed part of the Kingdom of Serbs, Croats and Slovenes, created by the unification of all the South Slav peoples. The progressive ideas and historical aspirations that led to this unification were betrayed, however, in the social and political order of the new state. The Montenegrin nation was deprived of its national rights and democratic freedoms. It was only in the course of the liberation struggle and revolution (1941—1945) that the foundations were laid for full equality within a democratic socialist federal community. The Montenegrin people made a major contribution to this struggle.

A general uprising against the occupiers was launched in Montenegro with the first actions by Partisan units in July 1941. Together with the other Yugoslav peoples, the Montenegrins won their liberty after almost four years of bitter fighting, and Montenegro became one of the six equal republics of the Yugoslav federation.

For centuries the Montenegrins had neither the time nor the conditions to write down their history: it was mostly preserved in oral traditions, and only fragmentarily in the writings of individuals. But this war-torn land with its spectacular scenery and the distinctive way of life and behaviour of its people, inspired others to write about it. At first these were mainly the travel chronicles of those adventurous spirits whom curiosity (and sometimes business) brought to this remote region. Later, particularly after the Congress of Berlin (1878), which recognised Montenegro as a sovereign state, reports and articles on it appeared frequently in the world press.

Since Montenegro occupied a strategically important area in the Balkans, various powers set their sights on it,

188. *Cetinje monastery, built in 1701, in the time of Vladika Danilo Petrović, was long the political, religious and cultural centre of Montenegro. Like its predecessor, the monastery of Ivan Crnojević, which has not been preserved, it was badly damaged during Turkish incursions (in 1714 and 1785).*

189. *Salon in the residence of the last ruler of Montenegro, Nikola I Petrović, who reigned until 1918. This modest "palace", raised in 1867 close to Cetinje monastery, now houses the State Museum.*

190. *Ostrog monastery, built with great ingenuity and skill into the face of a sheer cliff above the river Zeta near Danilovgrad. It has two small churches, the upper one raised in a cave in 1665, and the lower church, probably from the early 18th century.*

191. *The area of the port and holiday resort of Bar, on the southernmost part of the Yugoslav Adriatic coast, was inhabited in Illyrian, Roman and Byzantine times. Close to the new town of Bar stand the impressive ruins of Old Bar (Antivari), an important stronghold of the medieval Serbian state. Its ruined churches and other buildings, still enclosed by mighty walls, have the fascination of all abandoned places.*

192. *Part of the archaeological site of the Roman town of Doclea, named after the Illyrian tribe that inhabited this region, later called Duklja. The city was located at the confluence of the Zeta and Morača rivers, not far from present-day Titograd.*

193. *Morača monastery was built in 1251/52 in a wider part of the Morača river canyon, at the foot of Mts. Stošac (2,140 m) and Maganik (2,139 m). Raised by Prince Stefan, grandson of Stefan Nemanja, founder of the medieval Serbian state, it was restored in the 16th and 17th centuries.*

91

92

195

196

197

194. *The frescoes of the two churches of Morača monastery date from several periods from the 13th century on. Those from the 17th century rank among the finest of their age.*

In the picture: a 17th-century fresco of St George on the façade of the church of the Assumption of Morača monastery.

195. *Titograd, capital of Montenegro, lies in the Zeta lowlands on the banks of the rivers Ribnica and Morača. Mention is made of Ribnica in the earliest Serbian writings as the birthplace of Stefan Nemanja. A settlement on this site named Podgorica is first mentioned in 1326.*

196. *In the past four decades Titograd has risen from the ruins of old Podgorica, razed to the ground in bombing in 1944. Today it is a modern city with 132,000 inhabitants.*

197. *Just a few buildings from the period of Turkish rule over Podgorica have survived in present-day Titograd.*

In the picture: the clock-tower in the Stara varoš (Old Town) part of Titograd.

198. *The Podgorica Hotel in Titograd, its architecture well integrated with the natural surroundings.*

199. *Rising from ruins, Titograd has taken shape as a harmonious architectural whole with its modern buildings, wide streets, squares and riverside promenades.*

In the picture: part of the town across the Morača.

200. *The ruins of the fortress of Žabljak on the shore of Lake Skadar. Once the seat of the Crnojević rulers of Zeta (Montenegro), it was a stronghold against the Turks until its capture in 1487. In the late 18th and 19th centuries several battles were fought here, with the Montenegrins attempting to recapture their ancient capital. The church of St George with — in the citadel was turned by the Turks into a mosque, now destroyed.*

attempting to gain control by military conquest or diplomatic ploys. In their long and unequal struggle for independence and the preservation of their freedom, the Montenegrins increasingly realised the need for unification of their clans and gained a sense of national identity.

The constant warfare, harsh conditions of life, economic backwardness and inter-clan disputes often obstructed the endeavours of more farsighted people to foster a spirit of national unity and broaden the cultural horizons by opening up to the world. The land in which originated the famous Chronicle of Father Dukljanin (in Bar, probably in the 11th century) and the celebrated Miroslav Gospel (at Bijelo Polje in the 12th century) had to wait centuries for its first authentic literary work of genius about itself — "Mountain Wreath" (*Gorski vijenac*), by the great Montenegrin poet and ruler, Vladika Petar II Petrović Njegoš (1813—1851). This epic poem celebrating the heroism and love of freedom of the Montenegrin people was to be listened to and learnt by heart much more than read, for at that time only one person in fifty was literate. It was in Montenegro, as early as 1493, that the Crnojević printing press produced the first printed book of the South Slavs, but almost four centuries later, in defence of their liberty, the Montenegrins had to melt down the letters of another press and remove the lead roof of Njegoš' "palace" — the Biljarda — in order to make rifle shot.

Historical and geographical conditions account for the great differences to be found on the territory of present-day Montenegro. On the littoral, particularly in and around Kotor, education and culture early on attained a much higher level: literature was written in Latin and later in the national tongue; painters decorated the walls and vaults of many churches (and even homes). In the town of Kotor, whose cathedral was raised in the 12th century, there was a grammar school in the 13th century, and a theatre was founded in the early 19th century.

In the barren uplands and highlands, threatened by the Turks, the continual warfare and hardships of life checked any such development. Centuries had to pass before attention was turned to education and cultural activities, which thereafter made rapid progress.

Cetinje, under Mt. Lovćen (a national park), with the mausoleum of Njegoš (the work of Ivan Meštrović) on its peak, is a town of historical monuments. Its museums house collections of inestimable value. The old monastery has a rich treasury. A dozen buildings in different architectural styles are still popularly known by names recalling their former use. These were the consulates of the states whose diplomatic recognition was warmly welcomed by tiny Montenegro. Many noted artists, scholars and other public figures from various parts of Yugoslavia lived and worked here, hospitably received by freedom-loving Cetinje.

In prewar Yugoslavia, Montenegro remained poor and underdeveloped. The destruction suffered during the Second World War, from which Montenegro emerged totally devastated and impoverished, compounded the economic problems.

The postwar period has been an era of steady modernisation in all fields of life. The development of industry, tourism, education, culture, health and other services has fundamentally changed the face of Montenegro.

In 1979 it suffered a severe earthquake which, besides taking its toll of human lives, caused widespread destruction, especially of the old coastal towns and cultural monuments. By the efforts of the Montenegrin people, with aid from all parts of Yugoslavia and assistance from abroad, rebuilding and restoration programmes have been successfully carried out.

Today Montenegro makes a significant contribution to Yugoslavia's economy, having 25 % of its capacities for high-quality steel, about one third for aluminium production, 37 % for the manufacture of refrigerators, one quarter of its ship-building and 13 % of hotel and catering facilities for tourism.

The level of development achieved can be judged from the fact that every third person in the republic is employed, and that the share of the farming population has dropped from 72 % in 1948 to only 13.5 %.

The capital of Montenegro is *Titograd* (the former small town of Podgorica, razed by bombing in the Second World War), which has grown into a city of 132,000 inhabitants.

The Veljko Vlahović University in Titograd has faculties in several other towns (Nikšić, Cetinje, Kotor). Also located in the city are the seat of the Academy of Sciences and Arts, the Lexicographic Institute, the Josip Broz Tito Gallery of the Art of the Non-aligned Countries, and many other

201. *Sveti Stefan (St Stephen), a hotel-village on the Montenegrin coast, was converted from a virtually abandoned fishing village into a luxury hotel complex, great care being taken to preserve the original picturesque appearance. The village grew up in the 15th century around the chapel of St Stephen on a rocky islet linked to the mainland by a sandy causeway.*
On the shore opposite Sveti Stefan lies Miločer, a delightful small resort with luxuriant vegetation.

202. *The small church of St Stephen, probably built in the 14th century, when members of the Paštrović clan settled on the isle of Sveti Stefan.*

203. *The whole coastline around Budva, an ancient town on the southern Adriatic, is a series of bays with fine beaches, some very extensive.*

204. *Mogren beach, 400 metres long, is one of many which attracts tourists to Budva and its environs. These sand and shingle beaches are backed by olive groves and shady woods.*

205. *Budva, known to the Illyrians and Greeks as Buthoe, and to the Romans as Butua, is a very ancient town picturesquely sited on a promontory at the foot of Mt. Lovćen.*
Protected by massive walls raised by the Venetians in the 15th century and reinforced in the 18th, this is a typical Mediterranean town with narrow stone-paved streets and small squares.

206. *The village of Rijeka Crnojevića on Lake Skadar with its old stone bridge has a fairytale charm far removed from the 20th century.*

207. *Budva, the most popular tourist resort on the Montenegrin Littoral, is a happy combination of history, scenic beauty and modern tourist amenities which delights large numbers of foreign holidaymakers.*

208. *Since ancient times the men and women of Montenegro have expressed their need for dance and closer contact in their traditional "oro", a variant of the Slavonic ring dance.*

209. *Life in the rugged highlands and the strict rules of the clan have shaped the character of the Montenegrins. Proud, honourable, hospitable, tall and slim in build, they are the epitome of the Dinaric highlander.*

210. *In Montenegro, as in other parts of Yugoslavia, weddings are a time of great festivity and merrymaking marked by specific local customs.*

211. *Handicraft products displaying characteristic local features always attract customers.*

212. *Many Montenegrin households are still extended family units with several generations living together in mutual affection and harmony.*

213. *Mausoleum of the Montenegrin ruler and poet, Vladika Petar II Petrović Njegoš (1813—1851), on the top of Mt. Lovćen (1,660 m), where Njegoš was buried at his own request. The monument and sculpture are the work of Ivan Meštrović. The mausoleum was constructed between 1970 and 1974.*

214. *Perast on the Gulf of Kotor was once an important maritime town. First mentioned in the 14th century, in the 15th it already had a large merchant fleet rivalling that of nearby Kotor. The only place on the Gulf of Kotor that never succumbed to Turkish attacks, Perast enjoyed its golden age in the 17th and 18th centuries. Just off shore from Perast are the isles of St George and Gospa od Škrpjela (Our Lady of the Rocks), the latter artificially created by heaping stones on this site.*

In the picture: panorama of Perast and the isles.

View of Herceg-Novi, copperplate engraving, 16th—17th century.

cultural institutions.

Outstanding among the places of cultural and historical interest in the surroundings is the monastery of Ostrog, built into a cliff.

Titograd is also an industrial centre. Of particular importance are the aluminium works, building machinery factory and the agro-industrial complex.

Other sizable towns are: *Nikšić*, with an iron and steel works employing 5,000 workers; *Bar*, which with the completion of the Belgrade-Bar railway has become an important industrial and communications centre; *Bijelo Polje*, noted, among other things, for its woollen textile plant; *Pljevlja*, with several fine old buildings, such as Husein-pasha's mosque and Holy Trinity monastery, which has developed mining and power production; *Ivangrad*, with paper and leather industries, which is well known for its archaeological sites from the Illyrian and Roman periods and the 12th-century monastery of Djurdjevi Stupovi.

The coastal town of *Kotor* (included in UNESCO's register of the world cultural and natural heritage), the

232

cultural and economic centre of the lovely Gulf of Kotor, is famous for its massive city walls and gates, picturesque squares, churches, monasteries and mansions. It was the headquarters of the Boka Fleet, founded in the 9th century.

Tourism, an important economic branch, is concentrated along the beautiful coastline, stretching from Herzeg-Novi to Ulcinj, with its fine beaches, backed by olive groves and towering mountains, and clear warm sea. There are numerous hotels, some of the highest category, to accommodate the many foreign tourists who arrive at the nearby Titograd and Tivat airports, by road along the Adriatic Highway, by rail on the Belgrade—Bar line, or by the Bar—Bari ferry from Italy.

The northern part of Montenegro with its magnificent mountains, forests, rivers and gorges, is now more accessible to tourists. Durmitor — one of Yugoslavia's most beautiful mountains — attracts visitors in summer and winter. From the townlet of Žabjak on Durmitor a road runs through the famous canyon of the Tara, a clear swift river abounding in fish, the upper reaches of which, around Kolašin, form the Biogradska Gora National Park with the exquisite Biogradsko Lake set in dense forests. The Durmitor National Park is a nature reserve of exceptional value. UNESCO has included Durmitor with the Tara canyon in its register of the world cultural and natural heritage. West of Durmitor is the Piva canyon, 16th-century Piva monastery, and the Piva hydro-electric power plant, which has one of the highest dams in Europe. Another spectacular canyon is that of the river Morača, on the road from Titograd to Kolašin, in which lies the renowned 13th-century Morača monastery.

MACEDONIA

With an area of 25,713 km², the Socialist Republic of Macedonia covers one tenth of Yugoslavia in the extreme south, bordering on Bulgaria, Greece and Albania. Its population at the time of the 1981 census numbered 1,909,136: 1,279,323 Macedonians (67 %), 377,208 ethnic Albanians (19.8 %), 86,591 Turks (4.5 %), and 166,014 (8.7 %) persons of other nationalities and ethnic groups. (Another one million ethnic Macedonians live abroad, about half of these in neighbouring countries, primarily Bulgaria and Greece, and the remainder mostly in the United States, Canada and Australia.)

Macedonia is a land of alternating mountains and plains. Between the high mountain massifs lie fertile depressions and river valleys in which almost all the towns of any size are situated — Skopje, Bitola, Prilep, Titov Veles, Ohrid, Kumanovo, Tetovo, Štip and others. There are three large lakes of tectonic origin — Ohrid (348 km²), Prespa (274 km²) and Dojran (43 km²), two-thirds of whose area belongs to Yugoslavia and the remainder to Greece and Albania. Lake Ohrid is remarkable for its scenic beauty and rare specimens of flora and fauna, and the town of Ohrid for its many early medieval churches and works of art, which have given it a place in UNESCO's register of the world cultural and natural heritage.

The very name of Macedonia has undergone several shifts of meaning. At the beginning it was the name of one or more Illyrian-Thracian tribes living in this region; later it referred to the powerful state of Philip and Alexander of Macedon, and after the Roman conquest of the region in the mid-2nd century, it survived as a geographical concept, not always very clearly defined.

In the early 7th century, numerous Slav tribes began to settle on the territory of Macedonia, driving out or assimilating the previous inhabitants. Though they temporarily adopted the ethnic and state names of various Balkan conquerors, the Slavs gradually took the name of their land as their ethnic name, which in time, especially from the mid-19th century on, would be increasingly used as the name of a national community.

It was from this territory and in the language of the Macedonian Slavs that Byzantine missionaries undertook the great task of spreading Christianity and literacy

215. *The river Crni Drim rises close to the Yugoslav-Albanian frontier, near the monastery of St Naum (16th—17th c.), some 30 km from the town of Ohrid. Only a few metres further on it flows into Lake Ohrid, from which it emerges at the other end of the lake to flow through the little town of Struga.*

216. *In the mountains of Macedonia, where packs of wolves attack the flocks in winter, the Macedonian sheepdog known as the Šarplaninac (named after Mt. Šara) is invaluable for protecting livestock. This breed of faithful and courageous guard dog is becoming increasingly popular abroad.*

217. *Flower-growing has a long tradition in this region. There are few village gardens or town balconies without a colourful display of flowers and ornamental plants.*

218. *In the old days, members of the Mijaci tribe would drive their large flocks of sheep from the summer mountain pastures to winter in the southern region of Macedonia, returning in spring to the lush pastures on Mts. Bistra, Strogova, Korab and Šara. Sheep-rearing, which declined after the war, is now reviving, and the sheep's milk cheese made in the Macedonian highlands is a produce much in demand.*

219. *The fertile Strumica lowlands in Macedonia provide ideal conditions for growing sweet peppers, which are raised on extensive areas. The firm and juicy peppers from this district are to be found in summer and autumn at markets all over Yugoslavia, and are an export item in canned and bottled form.*

216

217

218

220. *Tobacco is another traditional crop which flourishes in this climate. Noted for its high quality, Macedonian tobacco, of oriental type, is exported in large quantities as well as being processed in local factories. It is the main cash crop of many small-holdings.*

221. *For family celebrations, church festivals and on other special occasions villagers bring out their attractive traditional costumes, carefully kept in wooden chests and smelling of sweet basil, the local substitute for lavender.*

222. *The Macedonian "kolo" dance is noted for its vivacity and complex steps calling for considerable skill and grace. Accompanied by the national instrument, the zurla, and drums, it begins slowly and gradually gains pace to reach a breathless climax.*

throughout the Slav world, from the Urals to the Elbe and from the Baltic to the Aegean. They were two brothers from Salonika — Cyril (died 869) and Methodius (died 885), creators of the first Slav alphabet, Glagolitic — and their numerous pupils. The most prominent among their followers was Clement (died 916), who in 893 founded a large educational centre at Ohrid that has rightly been called the first Slav university. Clement, among others, devised a simpler Slav alphabet, named Cyrillic after St Cyril. The autocephalous archbishopric founded in Ohrid in 893 was raised to the rank of a patriarchate during the short-lived empire of the Macedonian Slavs under Samuilo (976—1014).

Until the arrival of the Turks in the Balkans at the end of the 14th century, Macedonia was ruled in turn by Byzantium, Bulgaria and Serbia, with short intervals under other conquerors.

From the first encounters with mighty Byzantium, and later with other Balkan feudal states, the Macedonian Slavs resisted the destruction of their tribal way of life and the imposition of centralised government. Christianity was accepted, but not church institutions. This led to the spread of the Bogumil movement, which preached the equality and brotherhood of man and rejected all official forms of religion and the established social order. This powerful religio-polit-

Skopje, etching by T. Krizman, 1919.

ical movement spread further from Macedonia to many European countries.

Ottoman rule over Macedonia, lasting down to the Balkan War of 1912, brought five centuries of stagnation for the Macedonian people.

The general uprising that broke out in Macedonia in August 1903 — the largest and best organised of several rebellions — shook the Ottoman Empire and caught the attention of the European public. But the republic proclaimed in the small mountain town of Kruševo lasted only ten days and the rising was cruelly suppressed, with much bloodshed and destruction in reprisal. The division of Macedonia among Serbia, Bulgaria and Greece after the Second Balkan War of 1913, and non-recognition of the Macedonian people's cultural and political identity made the heavy burden of backwardness still harder to bear.

During the Second World War, Macedonia was under German, Bulgarian and Italian occupation. In October 1941 the people rose in arms and fighting side by side with the other peoples of Yugoslavia won their liberty. The victory of the Yugoslav anti-fascist and liberation movement finally enabled the Macedonians to become masters of their own destiny in the new Yugoslav state.

223. *Ancient civilisations have left numerous remains on the territory of Macedonia. The important archaeological site at Trebenište, not far from Ohrid, has yielded rich finds from princely graves, among them this lovely gold portrait mask (4th c. BC), showing the influence of Mycenean culture.*

224. *The world-famous icon collection in the Ohrid church of St Clement comprises some thirty medieval icons, the oldest from the 12th century. The collection is the property of National Museum in Ohrid.*
In the picture: The Virgin Mary and Child, a 14th-century Ohrid icon.

225. *The 19th-century iconostasis of the church of the Holy Saviour (Sveti Spas) in Skopje, carved in walnut, combines a profusion of plant and animal motifs with the figures of saints in local costumes. This realistic high-relief carving is the work of skilful craftsmen of the Debar area, who included their own figures in one corner of the iconostasis.*

226. *Heraclea Lyncestis is one of three major archaeological sites from antiquity (together with Stobi and Scupi) excavated on the territory of Macedonia. The remains of a palace with valuable, well-preserved mosaics, an aqueduct, baths and various statues from the 4th century BC and later show this to have been an important cultural centre and rich city, lying on the famous Roman Via Egnatia connecting Durres on the Adriatic coast with Salonika.*

Macedonian Motif, woodcut by Lj. Ivanović, 1934.

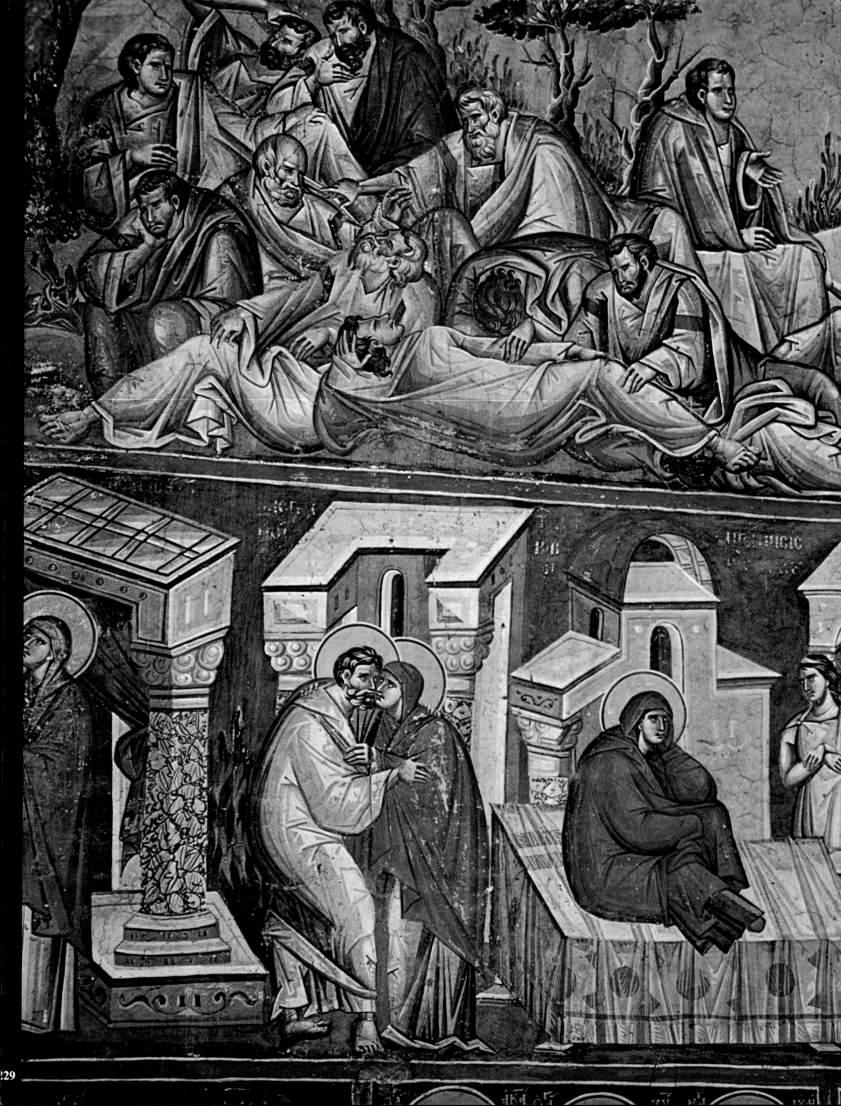

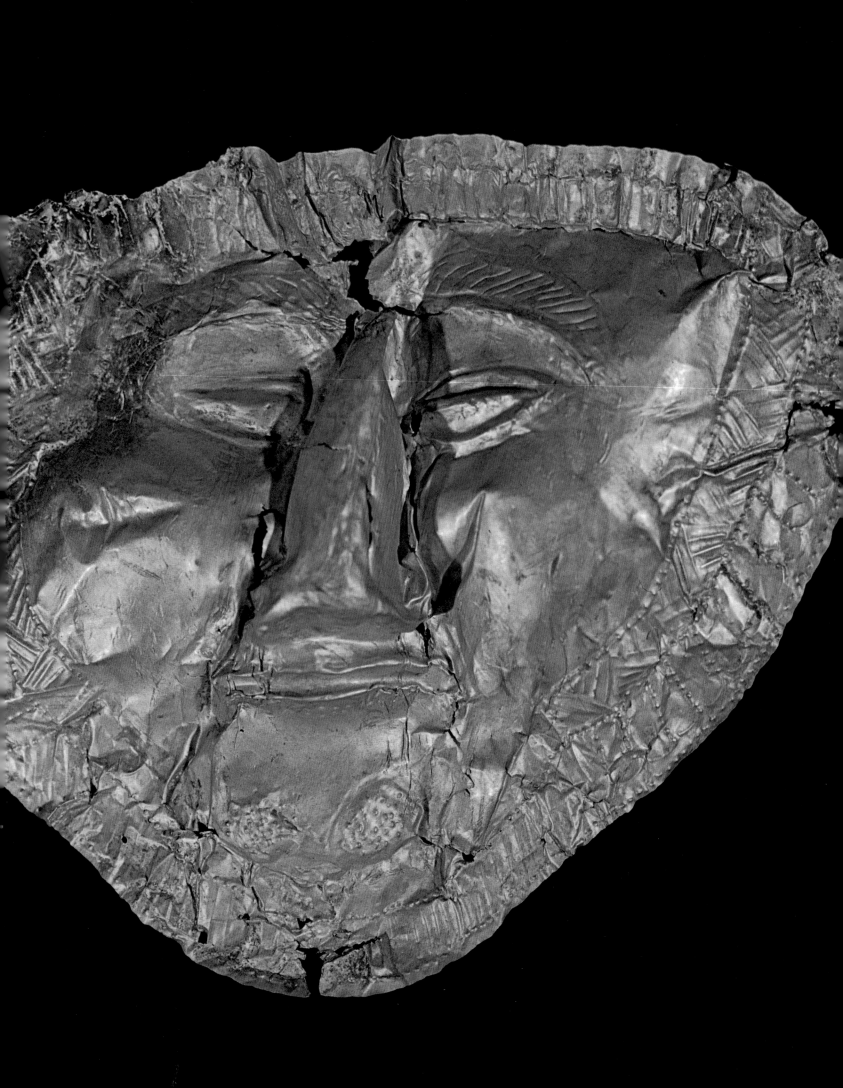

227. *The Colourful mosque (Šarena džamija) in Tetovo was built in the 17th century in the early Istanbul style, characterised by emphasis on size and space. It gained its name from its attractive façade in multi-coloured stone.*

228. *The Macedonian Orthodox Church gained autonomous status in 1967. Its head is at the same time archbishop of Ohrid. Thus, exactly two centuries after the previously autonomous Ohrid see was incorporated in the Ecumenical Patriarchate of Constantinople (Istanbul) in 1767, the Macedonian Church regained its independence.*

229. *The frescoes in the church of St Clement (originally dedicated to the Virgin Periblepta) in Ohrid are the work of Michael and Eutyches, outstanding artists working in the late 13th and early 14th centuries. These paintings, from 1295, marked the genesis of a new style in Byzantine art known as the Palaeologue renaissance.*

In the picture: detail of a fresco from 1295.

230. *The church of St John the Divine at Kaneo was built and decorated with frescoes in the 13th century. Standing on a bluff, in one of the loveliest spots on the shore of Lake Ohrid, it is a harmonious structure, cruciform in plan, with a decorative façade and dome. The unknown architect seems to have been influenced by Armenian churches in designing the octagonal dome with its ribbed triangular arcading.*

The whole postwar life of this old/new nation is imbued with a sense of urgency, to make up for the time lost in the long centuries of backwardness and barely perceptible change. In the period from 1947 to 1984, production has risen at an average annual rate of 6.7 %, resulting in an eightfold increase of the gross material product compared with the immediate postwar period. Industry has grown at a high annual rate, and has become the major factor in the republic's overall development, accounting for almost half of the GMP. This part of Yugoslavia has considerable mineral wealth: iron, lead, zinc and nickel, and is one of the richest in non-metallic minerals.

In agriculture, Macedonia is notable as the only producer in Yugoslavia of cotton, rice and early vegetables, and as a large-scale supplier of tobacco, grapes and various other fruit. Several large irrigation systems have been constructed serving about 20 % of the arable land. The biggest is in the Pelagonian Plain around Bitola and Prilep.

The republic engages in foreign trade with 70 countries, the greatest volume being within Europe. It exports ferrous metal goods, and products of the engineering, chemical, textile, tobacco and footwear industries.

Tremendous progress has been made in the field of education. In addition to a network of over 1,000 primary and secondary schools, there are two university centres — Skopje and Bitola — with 38 faculties, colleges of university level and scientific institutes. The republic has its own Academy of Sciences and Arts. Thus, in just a few years, Macedonia has travelled centuries — from the writing of the first Macedonian language primer to the foundation of an academy of science.

Numerous museums, art galleries, theatres and cultural centres in the major towns bear witness to the rapid flowering of creativity in the arts. About 40 cultural events, some of which have gained an international reputation, are staged annually in this republic. One such is the Struga Poetry Evenings, held every summer in the small town of Struga on Lake Ohrid, which gathers poets from all parts of the world. The town of Ohrid organises an annual summer programme of theatrical and musical performances, which includes internationally-famous names. Skopje has for many years organised the World Gallery of Cartoons.

Skopje (pop. 505,000), the capital of Macedonia, which was struck by a catastrophic earthquake in 1963, lies on the upper course of the river Vardar, on the Belgrade—Athens highway and railway. The city also has an airport.

The rapid reconstruction of Skopje after the 1963 earthquake gave the city a new appearance, with broad avenues and abundant greenery. Following the idea of the Japanese urban planner Kenzo Tanga, the centre was given a "city wall" of high-rise buildings, while the banks of the Vardar were laid out as pleasant tree-lined promenades. The ancient trading quarter (*čaršija*) has been completely renovated, but has preserved all the notable features of its original architecture. In this setting the old buildings of cultural and historical interest are seen to even better advantage. They include the Kale Fortress raised in the 6th century (its present appearance dates from the Turkish period), the Stone Bridge (15th c.), Daut-pasha's baths (15th c., now the Art Gallery), Mustafa-pasha's mosque (15th c.) and Holy Saviour church (17th c.) with a remarkable carved wooden iconostasis. On the slopes of nearby Mt. Vodna stands the famous church of St Panteleimon from 1164, decorated with frescoes of exceptional artistic value.

Ohrid (ancient Lichnydos) is a leading tourist centre on the shore of beautiful Lake Ohrid. The old part of the town preserves picturesque old houses in an original style, the ruins of Samuilo's Fortress (10th c.) and churches built here in the 9th century by St Clement of Ohrid. The many medieval churches and monasteries raised here contain world-renowned frescoes and icons.

The Ohrid archbishopric, abolished by decree of the Turkish sultan in 1767, was restored at an assembly in Ohrid in 1956, and in 1967 the Autocephalous Macedonian Orthodox Church was founded.

South-east of Ohrid stretches the well-known fruit-growing district of Prespa and the lake of the same name.

Bitola, the second largest town, lies at the foot of Mt. Pelister (a national Park), in the Pelagonian region, Macedonia's granary. Close to the town are the ruins of ancient Heraclea Lyncestis (4th c. BC), on the famous Roman road, the Via Egnatia, linking Rome with Salonika via southern Italy and Albania. Buildings of architectural merit in Bitola include the Isak mosque (15th c.), the Ajdar-Gazi

231. *A curiosity of Lake Dojran is the ancient method of fishing practised in winter with the aid of cormorants. The birds drive the fish towards the shore and into nets concealed among the reeds in the shallows.*

232. *Some well-preserved houses in the picturesque local architectural style can be seen in the town of Ohrid. Built in the 19th centuries, these dwellings hang over the street, each successive story projecting further than the one below.*

233. *Ohrid is the leading tourist centre of Macedonia. In recent years, with the construction of comfortable modern hotels along the shore, there has been a marked increase in the number of foreign visitors.*

234. *A group of young architects make use of features of the old urban architecture of Macedonia to give a local character to modern buildings. The result has been many interesting designs that successfully combine tradition with a contemporary idiom.*
In the picture: balconies of the Metropol Hotel on the shore of Lake Ohrid (8 km from the town).

235. *In recent years, new roads have opened up unknown regions of Macedonia, particularly the eastern districts. All the major roads have been modernised, including the busy Skopje—Gevgelija highway, the main route to Athens, which passes through the lovely Vardar gorge and close by several interesting towns and archaeological sites.*

236. *Macedonia is noted for market gardening, and in particular the growing of early vegetables, raised in large greenhouses and dispatched to many parts of the country.*

237. *Fishing is of economic importance for people living around the three large lakes — Ohrid, Prespa and Dojran. Dojran is noted for fishing with the aid of birds.*

238. *The open-air markets are always thronged with people in summer, especially around the heaps of thirst-quenching watermelon.*

239. *After the devastating earthquake in 1963 which razed the centre of Skopje, the city was rebuilt with help from all parts of Yugoslavia and many foreign countries. Several internationally famed architects have left notable works here.*
In the picture: the Macedonian National Theatre.

240. *The stone bridge over the Vardar gives access to the old part of the city with its many cultural and historical monuments. Built by the Turks on the site of a Roman bridge, it has eleven arches and bears a plaque in middle stating that it was restored by Sultan Murat II (first half of the 15th century).*

241. *The old part of Skopje has a number of large buildings of oriental architecture — mosques, inns and baths.*

242. *Apart from the old part of the city, which has retained its earlier appearance, Skopje no longer bears much resemblance to the city ruined by the earthquake. It is now a town of new residential quarters, built as urban entities, wide boulevards, and many modern amenities.*

mosque (14th c.) and the old Turkish covered market — the Bezistan. Like Skopje, Bitola is a university town.

Prilep, in the fertile Pelagonian Plain, was the stronghold in the 14th century of Kraljević Marko, an historical figure who became a legendary hero of folk poetry.

On Lake Dojran, on the Yugoslav-Greek frontier, fishing is still carried on with the aid of birds, in the manner of the ancient Peonians, who raised their pile dwellings here.

The village of Galičnik in the Mavrovo National Park, in north-west Macedonia, is a centre of livestock breeding and rug-making which has retained colourful folklore traditions. Nearby stands the monastery of St John Bigorski with its famous carved wooden iconostasis.

The unspoilt scenery, rich cultural heritage and authentic folklore bring more and more domestic and foreign tourists to Macedonia each year. The leading tourist areas are Ohrid, Prespa, Dojran, Mavrovo, Mt. Šara (Šarplanina), Pelister and Kruševo.